Crime: Economic Incentives and Social Networks

Crime: Economic Incentives and Social Networks

PAUL ORMEROD

iea

The Institute of Economic Affairs

First published in Great Britain in 2005 by
The Institute of Economic Affairs
2 Lord North Street
Westminster
London SW1P 3LB
in association with Profile Books Ltd

The mission of the Institute of Economic Affairs is to improve public understanding of the fundamental institutions of a free society, with particular reference to the role of markets in solving economic and social problems.

A CIP catalogue record for this book is available from the British Library.

ISBN 0 255 36554 3

Many IEA publications are translated into languages other than English or are reprinted. Permission to translate or to reprint should be sought from the Director General at the address above.

Typeset in Stone by MacGuru Ltd
info@macguru.org.uk

Printed and bound in Great Britain by Hobbs the Printers

CONTENTS

THE AUTHOR

Paul Ormerod is the author of *Death of Economics* and *Butterfly Economics*, and, most recently, *Why Most Things Fail* – an analysis of the predominance of failure. He is currently a director of Volterra Consulting. He read economics at Cambridge, then did postgraduate work at Oxford. Paul began as a macroeconomic modeller and forecaster at NIESR before moving to the private sector and the world of small business. He was a founding director of the Henley Centre for Forecasting. He has published widely in the academic literature. His current academic interests include understanding economic and social behaviour with models in which agents have low cognition.

FOREWORD

The Institute of Economic Affairs has a long tradition of examining economic aspects of issues that are normally regarded as outside the field of economics. Crime is one such issue. It does not matter that the main influences on crime levels may not be economic or that the causes of crime are not economic either. Much can still be learnt from using economic analysis to try to understand crime.

Even where the decision whether or not to commit a crime is a moral decision, there are still economic influences that will determine the tendency or desire of individuals to commit particular crimes. If the opportunities for profitable criminal activity are fewer, if the likelihood of being caught is greater and if the cost of any punishment is more severe, we should expect crime levels to fall. Similarly, if the opportunities for profitable non-criminal behaviour are greater, self-interested people who may have few moral qualms about committing crime may choose not to commit crimes in practice. Thus there are economic aspects of crime that are worthy of study. These issues have been the backbone of economic studies of crime – for example, by Nobel laureate Gary Becker.

In this monograph, Paul Ormerod suggests a new approach to the economic modelling of crime. Traditional linear models, he argues, do not take account of social interactions. They are therefore not especially effective at explaining differences in crime over time and across countries. The author takes new developments in economics and explains how they can be used to obtain a better understanding of the major influences on crime and how they interact. Using some of the insights from Nobel laureates Kahneman and Smith, the author describes lucidly the development of new economic models of crime that take into account social interactions between different groups within a population. Non-linear effects are part of the author's model. This means that a policy that is apparently effective in one area of the world may not be so effective elsewhere. It may also mean that several policies, when applied on their own, may have little effect. But when the policies are used together, the impact of the group of policies may be greater than the sum of the impacts of the policies applied individually.

Perhaps the most important conclusion of Paul Ormerod's analysis is how little we really understand about the impact of policy changes. The author makes some policy proposals derived from his model: and these are important. But if social interactions are an important determinant of crime rates, it is clear that simply pulling particular policy levers may not have the predicted effect – certainly the quantitative magnitudes of the potential effects of different policies cannot be derived from the simple statistical analysis of crime data. This may be disappointing. But, as the author is keen to point out, it is better to have models that produce uncertainty about the quantitative impact of crime policies but are correct in the qualitatitive judgements than models that provide spurious accuracy but, in fact, point to erroneous policy solutions.

The IEA is delighted to publish Paul Ormerod's work, which

provides a major step forward in our understanding of the complex interactions that have an impact on levels of crime.

The views expressed in Hobart Paper 151 are, as in all IEA publications, those of the author and not those of the Institute (which has no corporate view), its managing trustees, Academic Advisory Council members or senior staff.

PHILIP BOOTH

Editorial and Programme Director,
Institute of Economic Affairs
Professor of Insurance and Risk Management
Sir John Cass Business School, City University
May 2005

ACKNOWLEDGEMENTS

I would like to thank two anonymous referees for their very useful comments.

SUMMARY

- Crime rates vary enormously between geographical areas and over time.

- An economic analysis of crime can help us explain crime rates: there should be an important role for economics in the analysis of crime. It is clear that incentives such as the levels of prison sentences and the probability of being caught do have an impact on crime.

- Nevertheless, traditional economic models do not explain the huge variations in crime rates over time. For example, crime rates are much higher today than in the early 1930s, despite greater economic returns from non-criminal behaviour today.

- Differences in crime rates across areas are not easily explained by standard economic models either. In large parts of the USA crime is virtually non-existent yet, in other parts of the USA, it is endemic. Crime rates in England and Wales are 250 per cent higher than in the USA.

- Modern developments in economics, particularly those by Nobel laureates Smith and Kahneman, can help us develop better economic models of crime.

- The economics of social networks can be applied to the analysis of crime. Individuals can be grouped according to their propensity to commit crime. Interactions between these groups can then be modelled.

- It is clear from such models that tipping points can be reached which lead to big changes in crime as a result of small changes in the variables that influence crime levels. The variables affecting crime interact with each other in a way that economists describe as non-linear – so that we cannot assume that pulling a particular policy lever will always have the same impact on crime.

- Models from network economics predict that the most important remedy is to reduce the flow of male youths into the category of people who are susceptible to committing crime, and to remove from the criminal population key figures around whom criminal life in a community centres.

- The influence of voluntary and local organisations may well be important in reducing the number of people susceptible to crime. Long sentences for prominent criminals will help remove the hub around which crime can often revolve. Evidence suggests that an increase in the minimum wage will reduce crime.

- Experimentation in policy may be important because it is not immediately obvious, from network models, how some particular policies will affect crime.

TABLES AND FIGURES

Crime: Economic Incentives and Social Networks

1 INTRODUCTION

Purpose of the study: background and overview

The most striking feature of crime is the enormous variability of crime rates, both over time and across places. This observation was first made by Adolphe Quetelet in 1835 in his book *Sur l'Homme et le développement de ses facultés ou: essai de physique sociale*. It remains true today.

During the 170 years since Quetelet wrote, an enormous amount of theoretical work has been carried out on the potential causes of crime. These range from the macroeconomic environment and factors such as real average incomes, unemployment and inequality, to characteristics of individuals caused by factors such as their family structure and level of intelligence. A substantial group of potential influences relates to the criminal justice system and factors such as sentencing policy, the probability of catching a criminal and possible deterrence effects.

It cannot be stressed too strongly, however, that the existing literature, voluminous as it may be, does not provide any firm, unequivocal guidelines based upon empirical evidence on the true causes of crime. In particular, conventional approaches find it particularly difficult to account for the huge variations in crime rates that are observed.

This study aims to improve on the standard economic theory

of crime by including the effects of social interactions between individuals – in other words, to allow for the possibility that individuals may be encouraged to either participate in or to desist from a career of crime by the actions and opinions of their peers.

The aim is to give a *general* description of the process by which people become criminals. A revised model incorporating social interactions is in fact capable of explaining observed wide variations of recorded crime data over time and place. A detailed description is available in the Home Office Occasional Paper series *Modelling Crime and Offending: Recent Developments*, published in 2003. In the Home Office document, the model is used to understand the massive growth in both property and violent crime that took place in England and Wales between the early 1950s and the early 1990s. The theoretical model itself involves a considerable level of mathematical difficulty. Readers of this monograph are, however, reassured immediately that this is written entirely in English, aided by tables and charts.

The remainder of the introductory section documents briefly some of the variations in crime rates that have been experienced. Chapter 2 refers to two recent major surveys on crime, and discusses reasons why the conventional approaches have had difficulties in establishing many firm results.

Chapter 3 considers the important contribution that economic theory has made to an understanding of crime over the past thirty years or so, and in particular the extent to which incentives might be thought to matter. This chapter goes on to discuss the potential influence of social networks, and sets out a framework of the more general model of crime, which incorporates both standard features from economic theory and the role of social interactions.

Chapter 4 extends the discussion on social networks and

describes how a model that incorporates the effects of these can generate very different levels of crime either in different places at the same time or in the same place at different times, even when the general social and economic circumstances are very similar in the two cases.

The policy implications are considered in Chapter 5, which also incorporates very recent findings on the implications given different types of networks, of the different ways in which individuals might be connected to each other socially. Finally, a short conclusion is provided in Chapter 6.

What has happened to crime rates? How they vary over time

One of the most striking characteristics of Western society in the second half of the twentieth century has been a dramatic increase in the level of crime. In 1945, the total number of burglaries and thefts committed in England and Wales was around 500,000. By the end of the century, this annual rate had risen to around 3 million, a sixfold increase. Between 1960 and 1990, the total number of crimes in the USA rose by a factor of four.

Figures can often tell the story much better than words, and Figure 1 plots the England and Wales data.

It must be emphasised straight away that there are formidable problems in comparing crime rates over long periods of time, even within the same country. Methods of data collection change, and perceptions of what constitutes a crime worth reporting change, so that the data are never absolutely comparable in different years. But it is hard to escape the conclusion, looking at Figure 1, that crime rates are now much higher than they were 50 or 60 years

Figure 1   Total burglaries and thefts, 000s, England and Wales

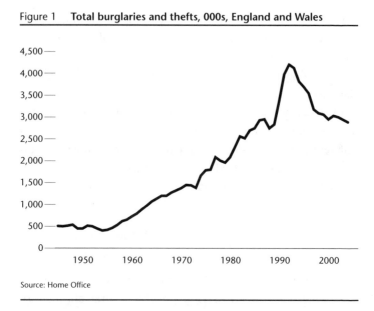

Source: Home Office

ago. There has been a distinct fall since the early 1990s, a feature also of American data, but even so crime in 2004 was very much more prevalent than it was in 1945. Crime rates vary substantially over time.

What has happened to crime rates? How they vary across places

A second key feature of the data – a 'stylised fact', if we want to dress it up in social science jargon – is that crime rates also vary substantially from place to place.

International comparisons of crime rates are even more difficult than comparisons of crime rates over time in a given country.

Figure 2   **Total number of crimes per 100,000 inhabitants, 2001**

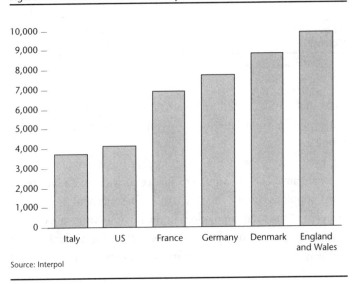

Source: Interpol

The concept of crime in, say, Albania, is almost certainly rather different from that in Aldershot. But we can use the latest figures from Interpol to examine crime rates per 100,000 inhabitants in a group of Western countries, all at similar levels of prosperity and culture.

The crime rate in England and Wales is over two and a half times higher than in Italy, and just under two and a half times higher than in the USA.

Confronted by this chart without the country names, and asked to identify countries from the list, many people, certainly in Europe, would probably place the USA at the top of the chart. But, in international terms, crime in the USA is low. The image of America as a crime-ridden society may arise from the very high

Table 1 **Crime rates per 100,000 population, US counties**

	Lowest rate	1st quartile	3rd quartile	Highest rate
All crime	4	2,078	5,198	22,320
Violent	2	121	513	3,584

Source: US Bureau of Justice

rates that are associated with a small number of inner-city areas. Large parts of rural America are, as an approximation, effectively crime free.

Even among the predominantly urban areas, crime rates vary dramatically. The US Bureau of Justice provides data on the 90 most populous counties on its website. These account for some 40 per cent of the total population. In the highest crime rate county, total crime per 100,000 population was over six times higher than in the lowest, and for violent crime the ratio was much higher, at over 20 to 1.

Across the USA as a whole, the range of crime rates from county to county is dramatic. Table 1 shows the overall and violent crime rates per 100,000 across the counties of the USA.

The '1st quartile' is the figure for the crime rate such that one quarter of the total number of counties have crime rates lower than this figure. So a quarter of all US counties had a crime rate per 100,000 people of fewer than 2,078 crimes a year. The '3rd quartile' means the figure for the crime rate such that one quarter of the total number of counties have crime rates higher than this figure. So one half of all the counties lie between the first and third quartiles. Even here, in the bulk of the data, there is considerable variation comparable to that which we see across countries in western Europe.

But it is the differences between the highest and lowest values which are startling. Indeed, the overall crime rate is more than 7,400 per 100,000 in no fewer than one county in every ten, and the violent crime rate is above 920 per 100,000 in one county in every ten.

The key features of crime statistics: enormous variations over both time and place

The precise details of crime rates and their movements across both time and place vary from country to country. But the two key features of the data are:

- large variations within a given area over time;
- even larger variations across different areas, all measured at the same time.

The challenge for the scientific and economic study of crime is to understand how such massive variations can come about.

2 BACKGROUND

Two major surveys of the literature on crime

A wide range of causes of crime has been suggested in the theo-retical literature, particularly for property crime. These range from the economic environment and factors such as real average incomes, unemployment and inequality, to characteristics of individuals caused by factors such as family structure and level of intelligence. A substantial group of potential influences relates to the criminal justice system and factors such as sentencing policy, the probability of catching a criminal and possible deterrence effects.

A huge literature exists. But a recent major survey by Robin Marris for the British Home Office (Marris, 2003) concluded that 'it cannot be stressed too strongly that the existing literature, voluminous as it may be, does not provide any firm, unequivocal guidelines based upon empirical evidence on the true causes of crime'. Marris examined some 300 papers and articles, ranging from some seminal sociological observations of Jeremy Bentham in the eighteenth century to modern mathematical papers up to the year 2000.

A similar conclusion was reached a few years earlier, in an American survey of the literature. Isaac Ehrlich (1996) concen-trated simply on the economic papers, which he noted were 'voluminous'. He considered, among other things, the impact of the criminal justice system, and whether making this more severe reduced crime. His conclusion was that 'it would be premature to view the empirical evidence as conclusive'. Ehrlich noted that the quantitative estimates of such effects vary, even to the extent of a minority of studies failing to find any effect at all.

The conclusions of these surveys by two distinguished authors may seem surprising. But they are by no means untypical of the social sciences. Economists, for example, will be familiar with the concept of the Keynesian multiplier. Keynes argued in the 1930s that a sustained increase in government spending would have a multiplying effect, as it were, on the rest of the economy. The initial spending would take people out of unemployment into work, so their incomes would rise, so spending would increase even further, and so on. Keynes himself regarded statistical work as rather vulgar, and merely offered the opinion that the value of the multiplier in the UK was between two and three. In other words, for every extra pound spent by the government, the total increase in national spending would be between two and three pounds.

The multiplier is a fundamental concept in macroeconomic theory, and once had a key role in economic policy-making. Yet, almost 70 years after Keynes wrote, economists have no real idea of its true value. The only thing they can agree on is that it is less than Keynes imagined. They cannot even agree on its *sign*, let alone its size, with some empirical models suggesting that once all the complicated feedbacks are taken into account, extra government spending actually depresses the economy.

The purpose of this example is not to enter into a debate on macroeconomics. Rather, it is to show that even within economics, the most quantitative of the social sciences, there is great uncertainty about the empirical value of a key theoretical concept. So we should be less taken aback when major surveys of the criminological literature conclude that very few, if any, absolutely unequivocal results are established.

Key reasons why research on crime is often inconclusive

Both Ehrlich and Marris address the question as to why research on crime has proved so inconclusive. Important issues in the methodology of social science are raised by this, which readily merit extensive discussion. But the full range and depth of such consideration need not concern us here. Instead, we can state briefly some of the key points.

Undoubtedly, the potential unreliability and non-comparability of crime statistics play an important part. Results obtained on a data-set particular to a time and place may not be replicated on data from another time and place, even if the 'true' levels of crime are identical in the two, simply because the recorded statistics may measure the levels somewhat differently. An obvious example is violent crime. Concepts of what constitutes violence in the first place vary from society to society. And what constitutes an act of violence reportable to the authorities may vary even more. For example, in many Western societies the level of violence within the family that is deemed acceptable and hence non-reportable has changed over the decades.

An issue that is more general to the social sciences is that of the great difficulty of carrying out controlled experiments. Very little of the data that we have in the social sciences is constructed for the purpose of analysis. Rather, it is collected for other purposes, principally those of government. So the police, for example, will record crimes reported to them and decide which ones merit investigation. The income tax authorities collect data on incomes in order to work out how much tax is due. Such data is not collected with the benefits to social science in mind.

Because we can rarely undertake controlled experiments, the result of any empirical analysis in social science is inevitably ambiguous. The degree of ambiguity varies widely from study to study. Undoubtedly, a substantial amount of research in criminology is at a low scientific level. In certain British universities, for example, a time warp can be entered. Criminologists can be encountered who believe in an enchantingly sub-Marxist way that property is theft, and that crime is somehow caused by capitalism. But even with the very fine work carried out using modern techniques, it is hard to regard any single study as being conclusive.

The lack of controlled experiments means that no single theory can be justified by data alone. Marris states this point very clearly:

> A theory must be capable of standing alone in both logic and plausible realism. If facts yield results that seem strongly to contradict the prior theory, either the theory is wrong or the tests are wrong. Social science is not in the position of Einstein who, when asked what he would think if observations failed to confirm his prediction concerning the perihelion of Mercury, said, 'I shall be very surprised'. In social and economic science we have difficulty judging whether results of observations are surprising or not. The problem lies not so much in sampling errors, rather in the fact that experiments frequently yield unstable results. (Marris, 2003: 11)

These problems can in principle be mitigated quite substantially, though not eliminated, by the use of what in the jargon is known as 'meta-analysis'. Suppose, purely by way of example, we form the hypothesis that unemployment causes crime. A number of studies exist which do in fact examine this theory. We can start by discarding those that are obviously scientifically deficient because inappropriate or outdated techniques of analysis are used. The remainder will almost certainly vary substantially in the details of their approach. Some will examine data in a single country or place over time (time series, in the technical jargon). Others will analyse data across different places at the same point in time (cross-section). Within each of these approaches, the studies may focus on slightly different aspects of crime, such as household burglary, car crime or whatever. The other variables used along with unemployment to try to explain crime will vary from study to study. Finally, even the definition of unemployment used may differ. A whole variety of definitions is certainly on offer, from total unemployment to unemployment simply among young men (who commit the bulk of crime), to attempts to distinguish those who are unemployed by choice from those who are genuinely seeking work but cannot find it.

So for a whole variety of legitimate reasons, perfectly respectable individual studies may differ in their results, and it is often difficult to pin down precisely why this is the case. We may be able to make some progress in understanding if we can find *qualitative* similarities in results across a range of different studies. The discipline of economics has made important contributions here, and it is to this that we now turn.

3 CRIME AND ECONOMIC INCENTIVES

Crime and economic theory

Economists are notorious among social scientists for their intellectual imperialism. Not content with thinking about the economy, in the last three decades or so their minds have turned to a wide range of social phenomena, such as the family and the decision to have children, and also to crime. Economic analysis of the phenomenon of crime was stimulated in the late 1960s by the distinguished Chicago economist and subsequent Nobel prizewinner Gary Becker, and a vast amount has since been written.

In orthodox economic theory, the agents – economic jargon for people or firms or sometimes governments – involved in any particular market, whether as consumers or producers, are assumed to act in accordance with the rules of what is called maximising behaviour. They are assumed to be able to both gather and process substantial amounts of information efficiently in order to form expectations on the likely costs and benefits associated with different courses of action, and to respond to incentives and disincentives in an appropriate manner. In other words, an individual is deemed to behave in a way that maximises his or her 'utility'.

The one thing these hypothetical individuals do *not* do, it should be said, is to allow their behaviour to be influenced directly by the behaviour of others. For agents in economic models are very dogmatic, with their tastes and preferences being assumed to be fixed, regardless of how others behave. This seemingly arid assumption has important practical implications, particularly in the study of crime, and we return to it in much more detail in Chapter 4 below.

According to this standard economic view of the world, crime can be thought of analytically as a market, in just the same way as, for example, the market for baked beans. This does not, of course, imply that there is a physical setting, such as the supermarket in the case of beans, in which crime is traded. People cannot go out and put a can of, say, bank robberies in their trolley and pay for it at the till. But it does mean that the behaviour of those involved in crime, whether criminals, law enforcers, purchasers of stolen goods or victims, is coordinated through adjustments in relative prices, manifesting itself through the size of the likely benefits compared with the likely costs.

The decision whether or not to participate in crime is made, coolly and rationally, by weighing up the costs and benefits. The benefit is obviously the gains from the proceeds of crime, while the costs include the actual costs incurred in carrying out a crime (such as the purchase of a crowbar by a burglar), the probability of being caught and the prospective penalty if convicted. In this model, punishment by the criminal justice system can be thought of as a tax on the supply of crime, which increases the cost and hence reduces the amount supplied.

This view of crime as the outcome of a rational assessment by individuals of the relative costs and benefits involved is in marked contrast to the tenets of conventional criminology. In this latter approach, the typical criminal is portrayed as having difficulty identifying and assessing alternative courses of action, rarely thinking through the consequences of actions, and not thinking about possible punishments.

The basic divergence of views in conventional economics and criminology on how individuals behave is at the root of many of the disagreements on policy. The probability of, and severity of, a prison sentence will have little effect in deterring many potential criminals according to the criminological view of behaviour, while for the economist its theoretical impact is taken for granted, and the question is then simply an empirical one of how strong it is in practice.

The role of incentives
The response of people to incentives

Conventional economics has many limitations, but the great insight of the discipline is that agents – people, firms, governments – react to incentives. This is as close to a universal law of behaviour as exists in the whole of the social sciences. Any account of an economic or social phenomenon has to take account of the impact of incentives.

For example, in the UK the authorities have installed large numbers of cameras to monitor speeds of vehicles on various roads. Drivers exceeding the speed limit attract an automatic fine. It is not certain that a speeding motorist will be punished in this way, because the film for the camera is costly, and the cameras are often left empty. Nevertheless, motorists who are exceeding the speed limit almost invariably slow down whenever they realise they are approaching one of these cameras.

Many of the other disciplines in the social sciences tend to be dismissive of the insistence on the importance of incentives in economics. I have noticed, however, that whenever I have been driven by, say, a sociologist or a lawyer, they, too, slow down when they encounter a speed camera.

Objections to the influence of incentives essentially fall into one of two groups. First, a belief that incentives matter is regarded as somehow being tantamount to believing in the efficiency of completely free markets. This opinion is particularly prevalent among other social science disciplines. Once one admits that incentives matter, in the next step it is assumed that one will be obliged to praise Lady Thatcher or George Bush, or whoever it is thought represents the hated political stance of certain groups of intellectuals at the time.

I raise this point not as a diversion, but precisely because it appears to be held widely. It is nevertheless quite wrong.

Economists often do not help their own case by their insistence that agents are able to follow maximising behaviour, or in other words to decide always what is best in their own self-interest. But this is addressed when I consider below the second group of objections to the role of incentives.

It is not at all necessary to believe in the whole of the standard behavioural paradigm in economics in order to recognise that incentives matter. For example, Ken Livingstone, the Mayor of London, introduced in 2003 a tax (the 'congestion charge') on vehicles entering central London during the day, in an effort to solve the problem of traffic congestion. Even the mayor's worst enemies could scarcely accuse him of being a gung-ho free-market economist. His political stance has always been firmly on the left.

Nevertheless, in a politically bold move Livingstone attempted to deal with the traffic problem in a major world city by the use of incentives. There was great uncertainty in advance, and indeed during the early months of the scheme, about how agents – motorists in this case – would respond. Many different forecasts were made. It is still not yet clear what the longer-term consequences of the scheme might be. But to date, the tax has worked *qualitatively* exactly as one would expect. Traffic flows into central London are lower than they would have been without this charge. This does not mean that in some way markets have cleared and supply and demand are in balance. It simply means that, faced with an additional cost of driving into central London, some motorists have decided either to reduce their visits to the area, or to use alternative means of transport.

So a belief that incentives matter does not necessarily imply acceptance of the entire corpus of conventional free-market economic theory.

Do people behave in the way standard economic theory assumes?

The second group of objections to the role of incentives focuses much more explicitly on the degree of cognitive ability assigned to agents in the standard approach of economic theory. Agents are presumed to be able both to collect large amounts of relevant information, and then to process this information efficiently in order to calculate the decisions that are 'best' for them.

In the context of criminology, this is a much more serious and powerful point. An important fact that we do know about crime is that most of it is committed by young men of relatively low skills and abilities. There does appear to be something inherently implausible about the idea that such individuals assess all the available information and choose the 'optimal' decision when they are, for example, contemplating breaking into a car or thinking about punching someone in a dispute in a bar.

The standard response by economists to such points is to invoke the 'as if' argument. In other words, while it may not appear that agents go through the process of finding optimal decisions, they behave 'as if' they do. There are layers of subtleties to this argument which need not delay us. But even the simple statement of the point is not as foolish as it might first appear. Very few of us, for example, know how to solve the difficult non-linear differential equations that describe the flight of a cricket or baseball, yet many players can catch one. It is 'as if' they had solved the equations.

But the evidence from other social sciences, and in particular psychology, is that agents do *not* in general act as though they had the level of cognitive powers ascribed to them by conventional economic theory. Within economics itself, the work of the 2002 Nobel prize-winners Vernon Smith and Daniel Kahneman has added a very powerful new dimension to this standpoint. It is worth quoting from Kahneman's (2003) Nobel lecture:

> economists often criticize psychological research for its propensity to generate lists of errors and biases, and for its failure to offer a coherent alternative to the rational agent model … psychological theories of intuitive thinking cannot match the elegance and precision of formal normative models of belief and choice, *but this is just another way of saying that rational models are psychologically unrealistic.* [My italics]

In his concluding remarks, Kahneman makes a statement that is almost ideally tailored to the question of how actual or potential criminals act: 'The central characteristic of agents is not that they reason poorly, but that they often act intuitively. And the behavior of these agents is not guided by what they are able to compute, but by what they happen to see at a given moment.'

In other words, the evidence points strongly to the view that criminals do *not* behave in the rational way that economic theory assigns to them. Most criminals would in fact be better off by getting and keeping a permanent job, even at the minimum wage. In general, crime does not pay. Criminals act more impulsively, paying less regard to the potential costs to them of committing a crime than the objective evidence indicates they should.

But this certainly does not mean that criminals fail to respond to incentives. They make decisions which, in terms of their own self-interest, are often not very sensible. These decisions can, however, be influenced by the various positive and negative incentives that criminals face.

Positive and negative incentives: what do we know?

The distinction between positive and negative benefits is an important one. 'Negative' incentives are those that deter and prevent crime – the probability and severity of punishment. 'Positive' incentives are those that encourage people to take up legitimate work instead of crime, such as the probability of obtaining a job at a decent wage, rehabilitation programmes and policies that help to provide strong, non-criminal role models for those individuals who are most likely to commit crime. A point of particular concern to Ehrlich, in the literature survey noted above in Chapter 2, is that the empirical evidence gives no real guide as to whether negative or positive incentives exert the greater influence over crime. And this distinction is at the very heart of the policy debate.

The existence of the impact of such incentives is, however, well established in a *qualitative* sense. It is not the purpose of this monograph to give a detailed survey of the literature – the Marris and Ehrlich work does an excellent job in this respect. Rather, it is helpful to note a few of the key things that we do appear to know about crime, even though their precise quantitative impact has proved difficult to pin down.

The first point, already noted, is that there is a very distinct demographic element to crime. Most crime is committed by young, relatively unskilled men. And the opportunities open to this group in the legitimate labour market do appear to have an influence on the level of crime.

The expression 'poverty causes crime' tends to be associated with those on the left. A blunt rebuttal is often made, along the lines of the Four Yorkshiremen sketch in *Monty Python* – 'When I were a lad, we were poor, but we didn't go out burgling, like these young people of today ...'. Yet just a little bit more thought reveals that the link between relative economic status and crime is an illustration, not of bleeding-heart liberalism, but of the importance of incentives. The easier it is to get a reasonably well-paid job, for example, the more likely it is that a young man from the potential criminal group will take this job and be satisfied, rather than turn to a life of crime. He may well still carry out the odd crime, for young men of this social status are rather prone to commit violent acts upon each other. But the attractions of burglary as a career diminish.

Perhaps the most powerful type of evidence comes from what are often known as 'area studies'. That is, the researchers examine the variation in crime rates across different areas of the same country at the same time. The studies can be extended to include more than one year, so we can examine both the changes over time in any given area, and the differences across areas at the same time.

In this context, the more specific and detailed the areas being examined, the more meaningful the results are likely to be. We might, for example, compare crime rates across countries at the same time, and how these rates have evolved over time. Certainly, in terms of conveying basic information, this is very useful. But this level of geographic aggregation is not particularly helpful when it comes to analysing why the differences occur.

There are undoubtedly many factors that govern differences in crime rates both across place and over time. Some will be of lasting influence, and some will be ephemeral. The aim of analysing crime data is to identify and synthesise the key elements that give rise to these differences. The larger the geographical area being considered, the more likely it is that important differences in potential explanatory factors might be averaged out. At the other extreme, if we are able to compare individuals and their crime activities, or lack of them, we can in principle not only find out a great deal about them, but each piece of data about how individuals differ conveys genuine information. Unfortunately, there is very little information in criminology databases at this very detailed level. So 'area studies' that use information at as detailed a geographical level as possible are used instead.

A graphical illustration of the evidence of the link between crime and positive incentives on an area basis is given in Figure 3. This uses data in the 90 most populous counties of the US, which are almost entirely heavily urban. In total, they cover some 40 per cent of the total population of the USA. The data, for the year 1996, are posted on the US Bureau of Justice website.

The chart shows the relationship between the rate of violent crime per 100,000 population and the percentage of the population officially classified as being in poverty. In other words, each of the circles in the chart indicates the data for a particular county. The vertical axis tells us the crime rate in that county, and the horizontal axis tells us the percentage of people in poverty.

The chart, apart from its own intrinsic interest, helps illustrate a number of typical points that arise in analysing data of this kind. First, there is a positive relationship between crime and poverty. High rates of poverty tend to be associated with high crime rates. The solid line in the chart is a technical way of expressing the relationship. One way to think of it is as showing how the averages in different areas change as we move across the chart. So, for example, there is a spread of crime rates across the areas where around 10 per cent of the population are poor: this section of the line can be seen intuitively as the average crime rate given this particular level of poverty.

The second point is that, although a positive relationship exists, it is by no means perfect. There is considerable variation in crime rates across areas with similar levels of poverty. While crime and poverty in some counties conform to the 'average' relationship, most do not. Overall, we do see that higher levels of poverty are associated with higher crime rates, but the connection between the two variables is imperfect. This is entirely typical of the relationships that can be found between crime and variables such as poverty. This may be due to variations in the specific characteristics of areas, such as neighbourhood watch schemes or the effectiveness of the street lighting. More generally, there will be other factors beyond these which account for variations in crime rates, which leads us into the third point related to Figure 3.

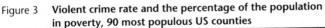

Figure 3   **Violent crime rate and the percentage of the population in poverty, 90 most populous US counties**

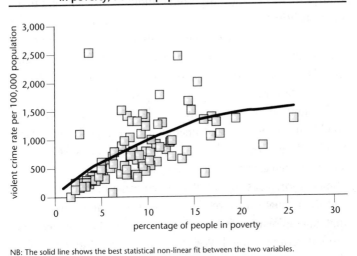

NB: The solid line shows the best statistical non-linear fit between the two variables.

Technical statistical analysis usually takes into account more than one factor when trying to explain variations in a variable such as crime rates.[1] But this rapidly becomes impossible to plot in a chart. The addition of a single further factor would enable a complicated three-dimensional chart to be plotted, but beyond this we have no means of representing the relationship graphically at all. Nevertheless, such statistical relationships do have meaning, even if we cannot show them visually.

A substantial number of studies have examined links between crime and a range of factors. As in so much of social science, most of the best work in this field has been carried out in the US. While

---

1   The relationship between violent crime and poverty holds up even when further socio-economic factors are taken into account: see Cook and Ormerod (2003).

one may raise doubts about or query the findings of any particular study, the fact that the most careful studies almost all point to the same qualititative conclusion is important evidence.

By way of examples, Allan and Steffensmeier (1989) use US age-specific state-level data between 1977 and 1980 to examine the relationship between property crime arrest rates (for robbery, burglary, larceny and auto theft) for juvenile (13- to 17-year-old) and young adult (18- to 24-year-old) males and employment conditions. They find that unemployment is positively related to juvenile arrests, but that low pay and long hours were associated with high arrest rates for young adults. Raphael and Winter-Ebmer (2001) focus on the link between crime and unemployment and use annual state-level data between 1970 and 1993 to show that unemployment is positively related to both violent and property crimes. Gould, Weinberg and Mustard (2002) look at the link between crime and both unemployment and wages in their analysis of US annual county-level data between 1979 and 1995. They find that although unemployment is positively related to crime, the wages of the low-skilled workers are a more important explanatory factor for crime. Indeed, they report that the falling wages of unskilled men between 1979 and 1995 led to an increase in burglary of nearly 14 per cent, a rise in larceny/theft of around 7 per cent, a 9 per cent increase in aggravated assault and an 18 per cent rise in robbery.

An impressive piece of work using UK data is that by Hansen and Machin (2003), published by the British Home Office. They carry out a careful statistical investigation, embracing a number of rather technical issues which need not concern us here, of property crime in the 43 police areas in England and Wales for the years 1992 through 1998. They find clear evidence that property crimes rose more, taking other relevant factors into account, in areas where wage inequality rose more.

The existence of 'negative incentives' also appears to be well established. The work of Hansen and Machin, for example, suggests that property crime rates in England and Wales are lower the more police officers there are and the more chance there is of being convicted for carrying out a crime. Other studies find evidence that the severity of punishment rather than the probability of being convicted is a key factor. It is worth mentioning one particularly ingenious American study. Levitt and Lochner (2001) analysed data across the US states over the period 1978 to 1993. They looked specifically at differences between juvenile and adult punishments for the same types of crime, and found that states where adult punishment is most severe have the largest decline in crime around the age of majority.

There is no need to go into detail on this matter, for the general points should be becoming clear. Standard statistical approaches can discover deterrence effects of various aspects of the criminal justice system, but it is much harder to pin down the precise factors that influence crime, and the exact strength of their connections to crime.

Incentives seem to matter. But the problem with this evidence is not just that it is difficult to identify exactly which incentives matter and to quantify their precise effect. It is that they do not seem to vary enough, across time and place, and with sufficient speed to be able to give a completely convincing account of crime rates.

In Chapter 1, two key stylised facts about crime stand out from the data. First, that crime rates can vary dramatically both across time in the same area, and across areas at the same time. During the second half of the twentieth century, recorded crimes for burglary and theft in England and Wales rose by a factor of six. Looking across places rather than over time, the overall crime rate in England and Wales is more than two and a half times higher than in Italy. And, at a finer level of geographical detail, the highest crime rate in the counties of the US, whether for all crime or for more specific categories such as violent crime, is several *thousand* times higher than that in the lowest-crime-rate counties.

It is hard to imagine that the effect of incentives, whether positive or negative, can of itself account for the massive variations in crime across time and place that we observe.

What else do we know about crime?

What else do we know about the causes of crime? A cynic might answer: 'Not much', and the cynic would not be far wrong. There is one point, however, which, after just a moment's thought, seems rather obvious – namely that the more things there are available to steal, the more are likely to be stolen. Vehicle crime rates were much lower in 1950, say, than they are now. But to a large degree this is simply because there were far fewer vehicles around half a century ago. Modern Western societies offer a veritable cornucopia of consumer durables – mobile phones, cars, DVD players, or whatever. Rare indeed is the home where these are absent.

We might usefully ask whether this contradicts the previous evidence that crime tends to be reduced when indicators of material deprivation, such as unemployment and poverty, themselves take on lower values. Surely, one might think, material goods proliferate only as a society becomes richer. So, on the one hand, the wealthier a society the higher the crime rate and, on the other hand, the less poverty – to use this as a shorthand phrase – the lower the crime rate.

The two views are reconciled if we think of the former relating to the absolute level of income or wealth of a society, and the latter to the distribution of any given level of prosperity. Relative as well as absolute factors matter. People live not in isolation but in society, and form views on their positions relative to others. For example, incomes after allowing for inflation have increased for all sectors of society during the second half of the twentieth century. But the distribution of wages at any point in time has varied over time.

The relationship between the prosperity of a society and the level of property crime is complicated by the intricate game that is played between property owners and criminals. A person may own an expensive watch, but he or she is less likely to be attacked in the street for it if the less salubrious parts of a city are avoided. A home is less likely to be burgled if it is fitted with alarms and security devices. To a considerable extent, such precautionary measures may simply displace crime elsewhere. This certainly appears to be the case with the proliferation of CCTV cameras in public places in the UK. Nevertheless, as any given security measure becomes widespread, crime becomes more difficult and requires more ingenuity.

Here in fact are the outlines of a biological game that has been played since time immemorial, between prey and predator. Criminals are predators on the property of others, be they criminals themselves or otherwise law-abiding people. Increases in the availability of prey, for example, increase the number of predators. But if the latter increase too quickly, the potential returns to each predator diminish, and some will be deterred. We can readily imagine the complex interplays that take place over time. And indeed, the mathematical analysis of such systems rapidly gives rise to great complications, even in apparently simple specifications.[2]

There is a more general point to be drawn from this analysis. From a purely conceptual standpoint, the idea, once appreciated, is fairly straightforward. Some may even describe it as obvious. But translating it into an operational tool, from which empirical evidence could be obtained, is far more difficult. The more realistic and detailed the description we are able to give of any particular aspect of the processes that generate crime, the more plausible it will come to seem. Yet, almost paradoxically, it is precisely the degree of detail which makes it hard to pin down evidence to support and quantify the idea. We can rarely, if ever, obtain data on, for example, crime rates in a particular street, the security measures taken by households in that street, the number of consumer products they have available to steal, the number of potential criminals who consider burgling these properties, and so on. It is at this level of detail that the theory is articulated, but data is simply not available with which to test it.

The same problem arises with a powerful and influential idea in modern criminology, which Marris describes as 'routine activities'. It was introduced by Cohen and Felson twenty years ago, and was built on ideas of 'social control' developed by sociologist-criminologists such as Hirschi in the preceding decade and a half. By 'social control' is meant those aspects of the normal socialisation process that will tend to help keep a male juvenile out of

---

2   Of course, many things are relative, and even the first few pages of a textbook on
      this topic would be incomprehensible to the non-specialist.

trouble. Hirschi listed these as, on the one hand, attachments and involvements and, on the other hand, beliefs. In the language of Felson the resulting social bonds give society 'handles' on the potential offender.

But weak handling does not of itself guarantee that large numbers of crimes will be committed. In addition, the personal ties of the neighbourhood are important. If neighbours barely know each other, for example, they are less likely to report suspicious activities.

Crime and social norms

This concept embeds individuals inescapably in society. The belief or value system of an individual does not fall from the sky like manna from heaven, but is generated within networks of people. It emerges from a complex process of interactions between individuals. Each may affect the beliefs of the others, and the collective ethos that arises from this will in turn influence the individuals, and so on. Equally, both the structure of attachments that individuals form and the social 'connectedness', as it were, of a neighbourhood evolve along the same complex lines.

This view contrasts sharply with the principles of conventional economic theory. Individuals gather information, process it, and then take decisions to best satisfy their own self-interest. And they do so in isolation. Their actions affect the behaviour of others only in an indirect way. A decision by an individual may alter the demand or supply for a particular product or service. This in turn, according to economic theory, will alter the price. So everyone else who is buying or selling in this market will face a different price, and their decisions will be different from those they would have taken at the previous price on offer. The interactions between individuals are indirect, through the price mechanism.

But in many social and economic contexts, individual behaviour patterns are connected much more directly. We see this most clearly in markets that are dominated by fashion. The market for Christmas toys, for example, often demonstrates very complex behaviour. Once it becomes apparent which toy is *the* object of desire, the demand for it rises simply because other people want it and are buying it. In other words, the tastes and preferences of individuals are altered by the behaviour of others. The demand for the toy of the moment does not depend just on its price, but on how many other people want it as well.

There are many other examples of this phenomenon. Financial markets are a much more serious illustration, whose behaviour affects us all. Basic economic theory suggests that the price of a share or the value of an exchange rate, say, is related to the fundamental factors associated with the asset or currency. In the case of equities, the profitability of a company is very important, because it is from profits that dividends can be paid. The exchange rate between two countries can be influenced by the state of their respective economies, factors such as relative inflation rates or public sector debt positions.

Economists argue among themselves about what in practice are the fundamental factors that affect financial asset prices. But, in addition to these, prices can be altered dramatically purely through sentiment. The shares of a company, or a particular currency, can come into demand simply because other people are buying them. In the politically incorrect 1930s, popular newspaper contests in Britain often featured photographs of girls in various attires. Readers were invited to judge not who in their own opinion was the most beautiful, but who they thought the majority of readers would decide was the most beautiful. Keynes famously likened the operation of financial markets to these contests.

Describing how such processes operate can rapidly lead us into difficult mathematics, but the general principle is clear. Individuals can affect each other's behaviour indirectly through prices. And in many contexts, they influence each other directly by altering behaviour at any given level of price. The price of the Christmas toy or financial asset of the moment may go up, and the demand for it still increase.

All this is directly relevant to the discussions above on 'routine activity' theory in criminology. The emergence of social norms that restrain behaviour and the development of community ties are both examples of the complex ways in which individuals can alter each other's behaviour patterns. People influence each other, and an overall set of values emerges from these interactions. The values in turn influence individuals, in a complicated system of feedbacks between individuals and social norms.

In trying to analyse and understand a great deal of social and economic behaviour, and in particular crime, we need to extend and modify the conventional way in which economics views the behaviour of individuals. Incentives *do* matter, and people react to them. The evidence for this is very strong even if, in the case of crime, it is hard to pin down precise quantitative relationships between cause and effect.

But the orthodox economic way of thinking needs refining, in two separate and distinct ways. First, in many situations people will not always gather all relevant information. They may not process it efficiently. And so they may not necessarily choose the action that is 'best' for their own self-interest. Instead, they may use much simpler rules of thumb to guide their behaviour. Second, their tastes and preferences may not be fixed, and can be influenced both by the behaviour of other individuals and by the pressure of social norms.

Standard economic thinking is a special case of this more general model of behaviour. Words in English can alter their meanings completely, depending upon their time and context. Since Chaucer's day, for example, the phrase 'bolt upright' has changed from meaning horizontal[3] to indicating an object that is vertical. In everyday English, 'special' has come to mean something that is distinctive, rather out of the ordinary. But in its technical sense it means something altogether less grand: 'special' means a restricted version of a more general approach. So Einstein's special theory of relativity of 1905 was developed into his general theory in 1917. The general theory encompasses the special but not vice versa. The special applies only under more restrictive assumptions than the general.

Overview of a general approach to crime

The approach to crime being suggested here has the following components:

- incentives matter;
- individuals may directly alter each other's behaviour;
- social norms can be important, and these can evolve over time.

---

3   As in the memorable sentence in 'The Reeve's Tale': 'as I have thrice in this short nyght, swyved the miller's doghter bolt upright'. Indeed, the word 'swyve' has itself evolved, keeping one of its meanings in the modern word 'swivel' but losing its alternative meaning, common in Chaucer's time.

If we assume that social norms are fixed, if we assume that individuals do not affect each other's behaviour directly, and if we further assume that people take account of incentives in the rational way that economics postulates, we have the special case of a theory of crime and human behaviour which is explained by conventional microeconomic theory. Conventional economics is by no means an empty box. But it is a very restricted box in which to work.

The problem is that in trying to move outside or extend the box, there are relatively few guidelines. The whole of the twentieth century was spent in formalising standard economic theory, and many seemingly powerful analytical results were obtained. The more general models of economic and social behaviour of the 21st century are still in their infancy. Daniel Kahneman, in his Nobel lecture in the December 2003 *American Economic Review*, concludes as follows:

> Incorporating a common sense psychology of the intuitive agent into economic models will present difficult challenges, especially for formal theorists. It is encouraging to note, however, that the challenge of incorporating the first wave of psychological findings into economics appeared even more daunting 20 years ago, and that challenge has met with considerable success.

It is to the challenge of producing a more general and realistic framework in which to analyse crime that I now turn.

4 CRIME AND SOCIAL NETWORKS

Why networks matter

The leading American liberal criminologist Elliott Currie gave the 30th anniversary lecture of the British National Association for the Care and Rehabilitation of Offenders (NACRO) in 1996. In his NACRO lecture, Currie drew the analogy between the spread of an epidemic and the growth in crime. His specific purpose in so doing was to offer a criticism of the American emphasis on incarceration, using the analogy that a health policy of putting all those who were ill in hospital would not be regarded as a particularly successful solution to the problem. Instead, the focus should be on preventing people from getting the disease in the first place.

The analysis of the processes by which diseases spread is conceptually quite distinct from the medical understanding of their specific causes and cures. Obviously, in practice the two are related since the discovery, for example, of a new vaccination will influence the spread of the particular disease it is designed to combat.

But for any given state of medical knowledge, it is important to have an understanding of, for example, whether a particular disease can be contained or whether it will break out into an epidemic. On a parochial note, Britain is one of the few countries in which the fatal disease of rabies is not endemic. An efficient carrier of the rabies virus is the fox population, and biologists have analysed the conditions under which rabies might spread, and how rapidly it would do so, in the UK. More dramatically, predicting the spread of Aids is of crucial importance to many governments and societies around the world.

The techniques developed by biologists for analysing these questions are highly mathematical, but rest upon a simple proposition – namely, that the spread or otherwise of a disease is fundamentally a social process. It moves from person to person, or animal to animal, by social interaction. The common cold is caught in a variety of ways, but only by being in close proximity to someone who already has it. HIV is disseminated by being in even closer proximity.

In a different guise, this concept of the spread of infections as a social process is exactly the same principle of interacting agents that we discussed above towards the end of Chapter 3. In the latter, the behaviour of individuals is influenced directly by the behaviour of others. And the same occurs in the biological models, with individual behaviour being influenced in the very specific sense of catching a disease from someone else. The larger the proportion of any given population who are infected with a disease, the higher the probability that any particular individual will catch it.

The techniques used by biologists to understand the spread of disease can be applied directly to analysing crime, precisely because we can regard crime as being in part an essentially social process. The more criminals there are in a given population, the higher the probability that any particular individual might also decide to be a criminal.

For example, the more it becomes socially acceptable for people to pay a tradesman cash, so conniving in tax fraud, the more likely it is that any given individual will behave in this way. We do not need to postulate that individuals are aware of the behaviour of the entire population for these effects to take place, merely that behaviour is affected by the behaviour of other people in the social network of each individual. These networks are typically on rather a small scale, comprising family members, friends and colleagues at work. So, in the example of the builder or plumber being paid in cash, his reputation for saving the client (and himself) money in this way will spread by word of mouth over small-scale networks. There is always the risk that someone will inform the authorities about these activities but, again, the more widespread the condoning of such behaviour, the less likely this is to happen, and the more the practice will flourish.

Of course, with a major crime such as a bullion robbery, the incentive to keep quiet is probably much stronger than the psychological pleasure to be gained by boasting about it in the pub, for the penalty for being convicted is severe. But the vast majority of crimes are on a much less dramatic scale, though this is not to deny that they can be traumatic for the victims, and the costs for the perpetrator if caught are not dramatic. So the knowledge that crime is committed quite freely among one's immediate peer group will usually be easy to acquire. Indeed, almost since time immemorial particular areas of major cities have gained reputations for lawlessness, where the social norms tolerate, whether through fear or the widespread participation of individuals in such activities, petty criminal acts.

Intuitively, we might feel that this offers a way to help explain the massive variations in crime rates that we observe across time and place. Such variations are simply not found in the incentive structures to which standard economics points us.

Sometimes, for example, infections do break out on a global scale throughout a population. In Britain in 2001, for example, foot-and-mouth disease suddenly became widespread in cattle across the entire country. Much more dramatically, the Black Death of the fourteenth century is believed to have killed at least one third, and possibly more, of the entire population of western Europe. On a less spectacular but still unnerving scale, the influenza that swept the world in the aftermath of World War I in 1918/19 is known to have led to tens of millions of deaths.

Yet humanity is constantly bombarded by viruses and bacteria of all kinds. Fortunately, most are contained in both numbers and place. Some, such as the deadly Ebola virus of tropical Africa, are highly virulent but do not spread into the population as a whole. Others, such as the myriad of varieties of colds and flu that attack us, remain confined within particular localities. And there are many whose impact is barely noticed.

The very wide range of responses we observe to how infections spread through a population arises precisely because they percolate through a social process of individuals being in contact with each other. The ease with which a virus can be transmitted and the scale and frequency of contact between people will obviously affect the extent to which an infection will spread.

Processes of this kind can give rise to what can be termed 'critical mass', or a 'tipping point'. There are textbooks in mathematical biology that run to hundreds of pages, illustrating the potential spread of many different diseases, with large numbers of examples of this phenomenon. But we can try to gain an appreciation of how this might arise. For example, if less than a certain percentage of a population become infected with any particular virus, it is likely to die out. But beyond a critical number – the tipping point – the chances are that it will spread much more widely. If a mere handful of people are exposed to a short-lived virus that is hard to pass on, it is very unlikely that this will spread more generally throughout the population as a whole. It cannot be ruled out in principle: the unfortunate individuals who are infected might, by chance, be extremely gregarious and have large numbers of social contacts. But there is only a very low probability that the virus will disseminate on a wide scale. But as the numbers who become infected grow, the number of social contacts of these people grows even faster. Very few of us go through the day seeing just one other person, for example. So if just one additional person becomes infected, the increase in the number of people exposed to this infection can be quite considerable. It is this which essentially gives rise to the phenomenon of a critical mass of people in the spread of a virus.

We can use this framework to think about how social processes such as the emergence of cultural and social norms, or the influence of peer group pressure, can affect the levels of crime in any particular society. It has the potential to explain large differences in outcomes. Some viruses are contained, others percolate much more widely. In the same way with crime, outcomes on rates vary dramatically across time and place. Sometimes crime is contained and remains low. In other instances, such as in a few American counties, for example, it escalates dramatically and almost becomes the normal way of behaving.

Combining networks with incentives
Population classification

The aim of our approach is to give a *general* description of the process by which people become criminals. Conceptually, the population – whether that of an entire country, a local neighbourhood or a particular age group – can be thought of as being divided at any point in time into a small number of discrete groups that differ in their potential to commit crime. In other words, an individual at any point in time is in one or other particular state of the world, defined by the propensity to carry out criminal acts.

As with any scientific approach to a question, this is of course an approximation to reality. Each individual is unique. But to understand the world, we need to make simplifications in our theories. We do this all the time. Think, for example, of using a map when out walking in the hills. The most accurate map would be one that is the same size as the area being mapped. All the minute details of the terrain could be included on such a map. But in practical terms it would be entirely useless. Instead, we use maps that try to capture the most important features of an area, and which leave out unnecessary detail. They simplify reality. In just the same way, when thinking about social or economic issues, or problems in the natural sciences, we attempt to concentrate on the key aspects, so that we can get a handle on the immense complexity of reality.

So we simplify and assign everyone in the relevant population into one of a small number of groups. In its most basic form, we can think of the population who are not in prison as being divided into four groups. First, those who are not susceptible to committing a crime (denoting this group subsequently as N, for 'not susceptible') – in other words, individuals with a zero probability of committing a crime. As a not unreasonable approximation, for example, most groups of women, certainly those over 25, might be placed in this category, as might most pensioners.

The second group is made up of the susceptibles (*S*), those who have committed only the occasional crime. It is very well documented in the criminology literature that young men in their teens and early twenties are particularly prone to commit crimes. Of course, by no means all men in this age group actually commit crimes, but they have a high propensity to do so, from acts of minor vandalism carried out in what used to be known as 'high spirits', to brawling in public, through to far more serious crimes. The rather disagreeable youths portrayed, for example, in *Trainspotting* show a remarkably high propensity to convert from being merely susceptible to being criminals.

The third group is made up of those who actually are active criminals, *C*. Finally, we know that at any point in time a small percentage of the population is in prison, *P*. These four groups, *N*, *S*, *C* and *P*, by definition make up the whole population. The approach can be extended and made more complicated by, for example, splitting the *C* group into occasional and habitual criminals, but the essential dynamics of the system can be understood by analysis of the simpler version.

The key ingredient of the approach is to describe a set of flows between these groups, whose overall effect describes the evolution of crime rates. A very detailed analysis of a model built along these lines, with empirical calibration to UK crime rates for property and violent crime during the second half of the twentieth century, is given in the paper published by the Home Office that was referred to in the opening remarks in Chapter 1 (Ormerod et al., 2003). Readers interested in the technical details both of the model and how it can be used to understand actual examples of wide variations in crime rates are referred to this, which at the time of writing is available from the Home Office website.

Of course, modelling the proportion of any given population in the *Susceptible* and *Criminal* categories does not necessarily describe the evolution of crime rates over time. In some areas, such as vehicle crime, the increase in opportunity afforded by the spread of car ownership has led to the typical car criminal committing many more offences per unit of time. But a description of how the number of crimes committed by each criminal evolves over time could easily be added to the model to give this information. Our concern is to describe the processes that determine the proportion of the population in the crime-committing categories at any point in time.

The movement of individuals between categories

Taking a snapshot of this model at any point in time, we would see a certain proportion of the relevant population in category N, another in S, and yet others in C and P. We might think of this as freezing the action on a video or DVD player and seeing where the actors are. We then allow the film to run, and see how their positions change. The first question to think about is: where is it reasonable for a person in any one of the categories to move? Again, we are making simplifications. So, for example, there are certainly examples of people moving from category N to category P in a single bound. Most murders – and murder remains extremely rare – are domestic in origin, and many are committed by a spouse goaded beyond endurance over the years, but who had hitherto lived a blameless life. But in general the first crime that people commit is not of sufficient gravity to warrant a jail sentence, so we can leave this particular connection out.

There must obviously be a flow between the N and S categories, for otherwise crime would simply fade away to nothing. Young men who were previously uninterested in crime are stimulated to commit a crime for the first time. Equally, there is a flow back from S to N. As mentioned above, a high proportion of young men, particularly from the lower social classes, commit at least one crime while they are young. But most of these do not graduate to become career criminals, and drift back to a crime-free life.

A part of the system that is reasonably well understood is the flow in and out of prison. A wide variety of approaches have been used to try to persuade prisoners to desist from a life of crime. Some offer positive incentives. Occasionally, these attract the fury of the tabloid press, when it emerges that a young thug has been sent on holiday, all expenses paid. Other approaches are definitely nuanced towards the more negative end of the incentive spectrum. In parts of the US, for example, prisoners may be paraded in public, dressed in fetching pink uniforms. But no matter what particular rehabilitation programme is used, the majority of prisoners soon reoffend and revert to crime. A minority do make an effort to operate legitimately, even if gradually over time some of these resume criminal activity. So out of the P category, people move into either N or C. And obviously there is a flow from C into P.

The final linkages are, first, from the category of occasional to more serious criminal, from S to C. Second, there is in fact a movement directly from C into N. Hard-core criminals do give up crime spontaneously. Again, there are many reasons for this. At its simplest, as a burglar ages and becomes less fit, he may no longer feel capable of squeezing through narrow openings, or of fleeing sufficiently swiftly from the scenes of his crimes. Also, the cumulative stress of being a criminal may eventually lead him to decide that it is no longer worth it. Many criminals operate mainly in their own local areas, and are well known to the police. They are natural suspects for interrogation when crimes are reported. They will often be in court and face fines or short jail sentences. The earnings from petty crime are rarely sufficiently lucrative to compensate for this. A further factor is that marriage and family responsibility may persuade the criminal to abandon his career. This was certainly a powerful factor in the UK over much of the post-war period, though the virtual collapse of the institution of the family among large sections of society means that this is now a less effective source of pressure. Yet another reason may simply be deterrence. A close colleague of the criminal may receive a particularly long sentence, and this is sufficient to persuade the criminal to change his behaviour.

The linkages discussed above can be displayed graphically, as in Figure 4. The circles show the various categories in which an individual might find himself, and the connections show where the flows in and out of any particular category take place. It is useful to remember that this is a schematic representation, and reality may be even more complex. But, as we will see, once we introduce the possibility that individuals or social norms can directly alter the behaviour of others, even an apparently simple system of this kind can give rise to complex behaviour.

We can usefully think of Figure 4 as a map, a map of how crime evolves in any given population. Of course, the precise extent to which crime grows will depend on the strengths of the various flows. But we can already use the framework in Figure 4 to start thinking about practical policy implications.

There is, however, another way of interpreting the schematic map. George Bernard Shaw's character Eliza in *Pygmalion*, on

Figure 4   Schematic of flows in the crime model

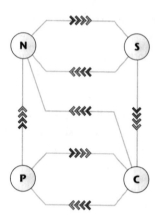

NB: *N* represents the proportion of the population not susceptible to committing crime at any given time; *S* those who are susceptible and commit occasional crime; *C* hard-core criminals who commit many crimes; *P* prison.

being instructed about English grammar, expressed surprise that she had been using it all her life without knowing. Non-mathematical readers may be similarly surprised to discover that they have just walked through a system of differential equations. For this is exactly how the geometric representation of Figure 4 translates into algebra. Such readers are reassured immediately that I have no intention of going farther down this route. But a word of explanation is needed. The categories *N*, *S* and so on represent a stock, the proportion of the relevant population in them at any point in time. The chart shows the flows between these stocks, or how the proportions in them might change over time. And this is exactly what differential equations do. They tell us how the size of any particular stock varies over time. The discussion immediately below, it should be said, relies on formal mathematical analysis of the system outlined in Figure 4.

How the number of potential criminals is determined

The next step is to synthesise the key elements that give rise to changes in the relative size of these groups over time. The flows between these groups are postulated to depend upon factors such as demographics, the impact of incentives such as the deterrence effects of the criminal justice system, and general social and economic conditions. The orthodox empirical literature on crime does identify such factors as being of potential importance, and the problems discussed above arise from the fact that the literature gives widely differing views on their relative importance.

Models such as that described in Figure 4 have, as we have discussed, been analysed extensively in a biological context, and a great deal is known about their properties. There are in fact some general implications which are of considerable practical importance when we interpret the model as describing the evolution of crime.

In any given time period, for example a month or a year, the majority of crimes are committed by those who at that time are in the hard-core category, the C box in Figure 4. Which of the connections in the model and which of the flows between the different categories are most important in determining the numbers in the C category at any point in time? Of course, the precise influences will depend upon the strengths we assign to the various connections, however we may choose to do so. But we can say two very useful things about the *relative* importance of the connections in determining how many hard-core criminals there are at a point in time:

- the single most important connection is that between the N and S categories;
- the connections between C and P, and out of P to N, are *relatively* less important than the N to S connection (see, for example, Murray, 1990).

Again, to avoid misunderstanding, the exact importance of these connections will vary according to the precise strengths assigned to them, but the above points are general properties of any system such as that described in Figure 4.

The connections between the C, P and N categories describe what can be thought of as the 'criminal justice' section of the model. They describe how rapidly criminals are arrested and convicted and then sent to prison. They describe how frequently people leave prison, or the typical length of a sentence. And they describe the success in rehabilitating prisoners so that they move into the N rather than the C category.

Catching and imprisoning offenders more effectively will reduce crime, as will longer sentences. So, too, will policies that lead to lower rates of recidivism. But the single most effective way of reducing numbers in the C category is to reduce the flow from N to S. This is not immediately apparent, and perhaps the easiest way to illustrate it is to imagine a hypothetical extreme example whereby, by whatever means, the flow from N to S is reduced to zero. Those in the S category would either revert back to N or graduate to C. Those in the C category would eventually either give up crime or be put in prison. And those in prison would either move into the N category or revert to a life of crime. But eventually, without a fresh supply of new *Susceptibles*, the *Criminal* category would empty completely. It might take some considerable time, but once the supply of new *Susceptibles* was cut off, it would begin to decline from its existing level, and it would over time disappear completely.

These properties of the model do not tell us *how* to bring about changes or how to alter the flows. But they do tell us that the single most effective way is to reduce the flow of those individuals (mainly boys) who become susceptible to crime in the first place.

This latter point brings us to an essential extension of the model in the particular context of crime, and the one that gives it entirely different properties to the conventional economic approach – namely, the influence of social interaction on the behaviour of agents. For any given set of external determinants of crime, the bigger the proportion of the population in any given category, the more likely it is that individuals in other categories will drift into that one.

Social interaction can be introduced in the model in a variety of ways. Two very plausible ones are as follows. First, the greater the proportion of people in any given population who are already criminals, the more likely it is that any other individual will convert to becoming a criminal. Second, the greater the proportion of the population who are wholly uninterested in being criminals, the greater the pressure on those who are criminals to become law abiding.

In short, in this simplified model individuals are assumed to form views on external factors, such as the overall social and economic conditions and the punishment structure, and use these to determine their movement or otherwise in or out of the different categories in the model. No presumption is made that they do so in an economically 'rational' way. But in addition, the absolutely essential element in this approach is that the behaviour of individuals can be altered by the behaviour of others. This social interaction between individual agents is crucial to the process of how crime rates evolve over time.

Applying the model

So far, this may all seem rather abstract. But a good test of the credibility of the approach is how it accounts for what is by far the single most important fact about crime rates. This is their enormous variability across both time and place. Even making due allowance for the various problems of reliability of the data, there are massive variations, even at the level of individual estates that are virtually next door to each other.

These variations are simply too large to be accounted for plausibly by differences in factors such as unemployment and the nature of the punishment system. Indeed, these latter often appear to have perverse effects in the conventional literature. A highly topical instance, which is frequently invoked in the current policy debate in Britain, is the contrast between crime rates in the 1930s and crime rates today. Unemployment and poverty are cited by many criminologists as being important in explaining the current high rates of crime. Others counter this by pointing to the example of the 1930s, when these possible determinants were much more acute, yet according to both official data and the testimonies of those alive at the time, crime rates were much lower then than they are today.

A more general example of this phenomenon is the wide variations in crime rates between the rural and urban sectors of poor economies; crime rates are often much lower in the poor rural areas than in the richer, urban ones. Elliott Currie (1996) attributes the low rates in the rural areas mainly to the community relationships, which both foster a sense of belonging and provide 'the setting in which informal social sanctions against aggression and crime can operate effectively'.

Our approach, which augments traditional economics with the influence of social networks, is intended to offer a general description of the process by which crime rates evolve. Its plausibility depends on it being able to produce outcomes in which crime rates differ substantially, whether over time in a particular population or when comparing different populations at a point in time, without having to rely upon large differences in factors such as social and economic conditions and the negative incentives of the justice system. Further, it must also be able to generate seemingly 'perverse' results, such as a high level of social and economic deprivation sometimes being associated with a lower level of crime than that which emerges in a more affluent setting. These, after all, are the key features of actual data on crime.

The model proposed here does in fact lead quite readily to results in which the proportion of criminals in the population can differ substantially, and in which apparently perverse behaviour exists. Assume, for example, that poverty[1] has a strong relationship with crime. Figure 5 plots that relationship.

To obtain the results shown in Figure 5, we choose a set of values for the other factors in the model, such as the deterrence effect of the justice system, and keep these fixed. We then solve the

---

[1] I use the term poverty here in a general sense of the word. It expresses a situation not just of lack of material well-being but the absence of economic opportunities in non-criminal activities. This is something that may well be an important variable in traditional linear economic models of crime and is used to illustrate the concept, although measuring the variable may be difficult.

Figure 5   **Relationship between crime and poverty**

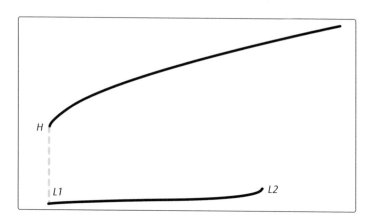

NB: Vertical axis represents the percentage of criminals in the population; the horizontal axis the level of poverty.

model repeatedly for different values of the social and economic factors. This enables us to trace how the proportion of criminals in the population varies with the level of poverty.

We assume that, in terms of the flows between the different categories of the model, as the level of poverty falls, the *qualitative* effect is always to reduce the proportion of criminals in the population. But the *quantitative* impact can vary enormously.

Suppose we start from a position on the higher of the two solid lines, at the very right-hand corner of the chart. From here, reading down to the horizontal axis tells us that there is a high level of poverty. Reading across gives the proportion of criminals in the population, which is high.

Gradually, as we move down the line towards the left, reducing the level of poverty, the proportion of criminals continues to fall. But, increasingly, for any given reduction in the level of poverty, the impact on crime becomes stronger. At the critical level, where the solid line ends, marked by the letter H (for 'high crime' levels), it tips the system into an entirely different position. This is indicated by the L_1 point on the bottom solid line, connected to H by the dotted line. So, at the critical point H, even a very small further reduction in the level of poverty leads to dramatically lower crime rates. Once we are on the bottom line, additional falls in poverty reduce crime by only small amounts.

But suppose instead that we start at the bottom left-hand part of the chart, on the lower of the two solid lines, and observe the effects of increasing the levels of deprivation. In practice, this could happen even if a society were becoming more affluent at the overall level, for particular areas or groups in the population could miss out on the general prosperity – as indeed seems to happen in many relatively prosperous societies. Initially, there is little impact on crime of increases in deprivation as we move along the curve past the point L_1. Nothing dramatic starts to happen when we move in this direction until we reach the point L_2. Any further increase in deprivation leads to a large leap upwards on to the higher of the two solid lines, joining it directly above the L_2 point.

This description of what happens to crime as the level of deprivation varies brings out the key features of the analysis, which in turn are reflected in the basic qualities of the real-world experience of crime rates.

First, even quite small changes in deprivation can lead to large changes in crime rates, as we see around the critical points H and L_2. But, more generally, the relationship between changes in deprivation and changes in crime is not at all straightforward.

The impact of any given change can vary dramatically depending upon the exact situation in which the change is made. Sometimes a given change in deprivation has only a small effect on crime, sometimes rather more, and sometimes a very large one.

Importantly, the *same* level of deprivation can, depending on where we start from, be associated with substantially *different* rates of crime. For levels of deprivation between the points L_1 and L_2, we can either be on the bottom solid line, and experience low crime rates, or we can be on the top line, and suffer high ones.

This complexity is entirely typical of many economic and social situations. We can *in principle* say useful things about what happens to crime rates when social and economic deprivation changes from any particular existing level. But the relationship between the two is very complex and is not amenable to discovery by conventional analysis.

This complicated behaviour exists precisely because of the presence of social interaction, the factors that introduce the concept that the behaviour of individuals can be affected directly by the behaviour of others. In technical terms, the interactions introduce non-linearities that lead to the existence of multiple equilibrium points. But the process can be understood informally. Consider, for example, what happens when we examine the consequences of making the impact of poverty gradually more important in the decision to become a criminal. Not surprisingly, the model suggests that this leads to a gradual increase in the proportion of the population who are criminals. This in turn, however, leads to feedbacks through the influence of the social interaction terms. As the proportion of criminals rises, this in itself makes it more likely that the proportion will increase still further. And the greater the criminal proportion of a population, the weaker the sanctions of social disapproval of the non-criminal part of the population, so the incentive to stop being a criminal is reduced.

Once a critical point is reached, the strength of these feedbacks intensifies, and the proportion of criminals rises rapidly and dramatically. This does not mean that everyone eventually becomes a criminal, for the strengths of the various flows in the model will set limits to the proportion that ends up in this category. But it does mean that two populations, whose circumstances are very similar but who happen to lie either side of the critical point, will end up with dramatically different crime rates.

Another illustration is given by examining the effects of changes in the severity of the criminal justice system, given in Figure 6. We assume that the effect of, say, a more punitive criminal justice system is to reduce the proportion of criminals in the population. The harshness of the system is represented along the horizontal axis, and the proportion of criminals in the population on the vertical axis. Imagine that we start from a position in the top left-hand corner of Figure 6, where a very lax regime is associated with high levels of crime. What happens to crime when the justice system is made more punitive?

As the criminal justice system becomes more strict, it exercises a deterrent on crime and the proportion of criminals in the population falls. But the effect at first is rather minimal. Greater severity does reduce crime, but not by very much. This is shown by what happens as we move down the upper of the two solid lines. Gradually, as we move along the line to the right, for any given increase in the effectiveness of negative incentives, the impact on crime becomes stronger. At the critical level, where the solid line ends, marked by the letter *H*, we once again

Figure 6   **Effects on crime rates of changes in the severity of the criminal justice system**

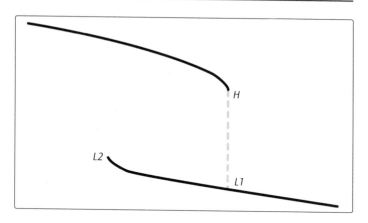

NB: The vertical axis represents the percentage of the population who are criminals; the horizontal axis the severity of criminal justice system.

experience a dramatic drop to the point L_1 on the lower of the two solid lines.

This helps to illuminate the current debate on the desirability or otherwise of the so-called zero-tolerance policy of policing adopted with apparently great success in several US cities. The social interaction effects in the model imply that large and seemingly inexplicable changes in crime rates can take place. Inexplicable, that is, within the conventional mindset, which looks for simple cause-and-effect mechanisms. If the actual process that generates crime were close to a critical level, the introduction of zero tolerance could shift the system to a new, altogether lower level of crime. But this does not mean that the adoption of such a policy in other cities will necessarily have the same impact. A city positioned in the top left of our simplified model in Figure 6 would see only relatively minor changes in crime rates as a result of adopting the policy.

The features exhibited in Figures 5 and 6 are an important reason why the conventional literature on crime fails to arrive at a consensus in terms of the impact of different policies on crime rates. With data taken from certain parts of Figure 6, say, the orthodox approach will work well, and show quite clearly that, say, longer prison sentences lead to lower crime. But, with other samples of data, the results will seem perverse. If a researcher were given data taken from a few points to the immediate left of point H, derived from certain places or times, combined with all the data to the left of point L_1, derived from other places or times, he or she would be forced to conclude that shorter sentences, for example, appeared to reduce crime, for that would be the information contained in that particular sample of data. There may of course be many other explanatory variables, all of which will interact and some of which cannot be measured by a simple index. Furthermore, some of the variables will not necessarily be capable of adjustment using policy instruments. In our simple explanations we have just looked at how crime may behave when two variables are altered and all the others remain the same.

A similar approach to the above was tested on US data by three innovative economists (Glaeser et al., 1996). They, too, note from the outset that 'The most puzzling aspect of crime is not its overall level nor the relationships between it and either deterrence or economic opportunity. Rather, we believe that the most intriguing aspect of crime is its astoundingly high variation across time and space.'

Their model is based on the behaviour of individual agents

at a very local level, in which there are three types of agent. The first two are those who are diehard law-breakers and those who are diehard law-abiders, neither of which is influenced by the actions of others. The third category contains people who imitate the behaviour of their immediate neighbours. The authors state that the first two types are maximising utility by making their choice, but this is not strictly relevant to their model. In one sense, the spirit of their model is certainly in keeping with our own in that it is not necessary to specify any of the factors that determine whether or not, for example, an individual chooses to be a diehard criminal. The model analyses the consequences once such a decision is made.

In the model described here, the social interaction is postulated to work at the aggregate level, with the total proportion observed in the C category influencing the decision of people to convert from S, but as Glaeser et al. note, 'ideally, a model might contain both local interactions and global interactions'.

They examine the spatial variation in crime rates in cities across the US in both 1970 and 1985, and at police precinct level in the city of New York. They find that social interaction is the key reason why crime rates vary so much, concluding that the amount of social interaction is highest in petty crime, moderate in more serious crimes, and almost negligible in murder and rape.

The application of the model to UK data

The model described above, and summarised in Figure 4, was calibrated to data for burglaries and violent crime in England and Wales, in both the 1990s and early 1950s (Ormerod et al., 2003). I give here a brief overview of the results for burglary, full details being available in the above reference. Over this period, the recorded number of burglaries rose some tenfold, from around 60,000 to 600,000 a year. The crime model is able to generate solutions that correspond to both these quite different levels of burglary.

A key decision in the calibration was to decide the relevant total population. Given that most crime of this nature is committed by young, relatively unskilled men, the study selected as the population the number of young men between 15 and 30 in the bottom quarter of the income distribution. In the late 1990s, there were approximately 1.5 million in this group, and in the early 1950s some 1.2 million. So a small increase in crime would have been expected because of the growth in this population, but this rise is very small compared with the growth in the number of burglaries recorded.

A key implication of the model is that there has been a very marked shift in the distribution across the categories (*Criminal*, *Susceptible* and so on), which in turn implies a distinct difference in social norms in the two periods. In both periods, those not susceptible to commiting a crime at any given point in time constitute the vast majority of the relevant population. But the percentage is distinctly lower in the late 1990s than in the early 1950s, implying very marked increases in those susceptible to the occasional crime (*S*), hard-core criminals (*C*) and those in prison (*P*).

A solution that is compatible with the observed levels of crime is that in the early 1950s some 97 per cent of poor youths were, at any given point in time, not susceptible to crime, but this percentage had fallen to 80–85 per cent by the end of the century. Of course, it is important to emphasise that this does not mean that 97 per cent of the relevant youths never committed a crime during their time in the 'at risk' group, as it were: rather that they did not do so in any given year. In fact, the particular solutions of the model imply that in the late 1990s a young, relatively unskilled young man had a 55 per cent chance of committing at least one crime between his mid-teens and early thirties, and in the early 1950s this was only around 30 per cent.

Membership of any single one of the crime-committing categories, even the susceptible-to-crime one (S), represented highly deviant behaviour in the early 1950s. These percentages are only approximations, but around 2 per cent were in the *Susceptible* category, and less than 0.5 per cent in the hard-core criminal category. Less than 1,000 people were in prison for burglary convictions. And, it must be stressed, these are percentages of the small fraction of the population that is far more likely to burgle than any other, namely young men in the bottom quarter of the income distribution. Even to express them in terms of the total population of young men, these percentages need to be divided by a factor of four. The percentage of the total population susceptible to committing crime was tiny.

So the overwhelming social norm at any point in time in the early 1950s was *not* to commit a crime. In contrast, some fifty years later, around 16 per cent of the relevant population committed the occasional burglary during any given year, and approximately 2.5 per cent – one in 40 – could be classed as hard-core burglars. The social milieu among the relatively poor has changed dramatically.

The above estimates, it must be stressed, are precisely that, and should not be treated as though they carried the precision of data obtained from an experiment in the natural sciences. But it is hard to escape the conclusion, no matter how the model is calibrated, that there has been a very substantial change in social norms among the poor youth of Britain over the second half of the twentieth century.

Assessing the contribution of individual variables to the massive changes that have taken place during this period is by no means straightforward, for they interact in complex ways. In terms both of burglary and of violent crime, however, the model implies that much of the increase has taken place because of an increase in the proportion of the poor, less skilled youth population that graduates to the category C, or hard-core criminal. This has very recently become a focus of concern for the government, with the identification in early 2005 of the social group known as NEETS (Not in Education, Employment or Training), though the crime model above identified this to be the case over two years previously.

As we have already noted, once an individual is in this category, the criminal justice system, short of truly massive increases in the length of prison sentences, has relatively little impact on his behaviour. In fact, the average prison sentence now appears to be very similar to its length in the 1950s.[2] The probability of conviction and incarceration for any given crime has fallen sharply, to around one fifth of its level fifty years ago, which would tend to increase the number of criminals, but the model suggests that this itself has not had a strong influence on the outcome.

The main reason for the rise in crime appears to be the larger proportion of the relevant population of young men who now spend some time in the *Susceptible* category. It is precisely this category which provides the recruits for the small minority of hard-core criminals.

---

2 Remarkably, the Home Office does not have a definitive series on this variable over a long period of time.

In turn, the increase in the numbers both who spend time in the *Susceptible* category and who are in the category at any point in time appears to be due principally to two factors. First, through the changes in social norms, which make criminal acts more acceptable. Second, the reduction in deterrence on the *Non-susceptible* group brought about by the dramatically lower probability of being caught, convicted and imprisoned for any given crime. Even allowing for contributions from the increased availability of goods to steal and from the increase in inequality, it is difficult to account for the sheer scale of the rise in crime without concluding that, qualitatively, the sharp reduction in deterrence has had an impact.

5 EXTENDING THE ANALYSIS: IMPLICATIONS OF DIFFERENT TYPES OF SOCIAL NETWORK

Overview

Our framework of analysis, stark though it may be in outline, has clear positive implications for policy. The complexities of the model are introduced by the terms that represent social interaction. It is the act of observing the behaviour of others and being induced to change one's own behaviour as a result which leads to these complexities. And this is such a basic and obvious feature of reality that it cannot be ignored by any approach that purports to offer insights into how crime develops.

Our approach, despite its underlying mathematical complexity, is in some ways an illustration of the old saying 'One bad apple spoils the whole barrel'. As Figures 5 and 6 show, it is not quite as simple as that, for the existence of a small number of criminals in a neighbourhood does not mean that the contamination will spread automatically on a wide scale. The trick is to keep society on the lower rather than the higher of the two solid lines in our charts.

The implication is that potentially by far the most effective way to tackle crime is by targeting social interaction directly. There will always be a certain number of criminals in any society, no matter how well behaved. Policies should be geared to minimising their potential influence on others. Prison has a role to play, but it is ultimately more effective to reduce the impact of criminals by promoting positive behaviour. For example, actions that reinforce respectable community values and which provide strong, non-criminal role models for those individuals who are at any point in time most susceptible to commit crime can have quite dramatic effects both in reducing crime levels in high crime areas, and in preventing explosions of crime in relatively low crime areas.

The analysis above contains an important assumption, which is not at all obvious. One might be tempted to say 'conceals' rather than 'contains', except that I am about to make it explicit. A view is taken on the structure of the social network that connects individuals. In other words, which individuals are likely to come into contact with each other?

In the discussion above, the assumption is made that each person is as likely to be influenced by any given individual as any other. In describing the spread of the common cold, for example, this might be a reasonable simplification to make. There is no need to be in particularly intimate contact with someone in order to catch their cold. Travelling around on our day-to-day business, going to work, going shopping, and so on, we encounter people at random. And those infected with a cold might pass it on to us, even though we may never come across them again.

We can readily imagine a variety of different types of social network in which individuals might affect each other's behaviour. In a densely knit community, for example, most people will know each other's business and know what everyone else is up to. At the other extreme, the community may be highly fragmented, not necessarily in a geographical sense, with individuals having very few social contacts, leading rather isolated lives. Yet another possible structure is one in which most people are potentially influenced by only a small number of others, but a few people are well known to many others.

There is an entire branch of mathematics, known perhaps confusingly as 'graph theory', which describes the implications of different ways in which objects – in this case people – are connected to each other. In the past few years, there has been an explosion of interest in the application of this approach to social and economic issues. One of the main focuses, and probably the principal one to date, has been precisely the questions of how viruses or ideas percolate across a social network in which individuals influence each other, and of what a good inoculation strategy might be in different types of network.

The basic principle, that the influence of the social network is of decisive importance in understanding social and economic outcomes, remains the same almost regardless of the type of network that we might believe applies in any particular situation. But the strategies we might adopt to use the network structure to alter outcomes will vary.

The analysis of social networks has attracted people from a variety of disciplines: statistical physicists, mathematicians, highly numerate US sociologists, though hardly any economists. This is perhaps not surprising, given the emphasis in economic theory on people behaving in isolation, like Robinson Crusoe, and interacting with each other only indirectly via the price mechanism. Yet when combined with the unique insight of economics on the importance of incentives, the analysis has the potential to increase dramatically our understanding of the economic and social world.

Scale-free networks: why they are different

We noted above a type of network in which most people are potentially influenced by only a small number of others, but a few people are well known to many others. It turns out that this is typical of many real-world social and economic networks. In its pure, theoretical form it is known, for reasons that need not detain us, as a 'scale-free network'.

Of course, actual networks are never absolutely identical to their Platonic idea in theory. But a number of well-known networks look very similar to the scale-free networks of graph theory, such as the World Wide Web. Casual empiricism – or everyday experience, to strip the phrase of its social science jargon – suggests that this seems reasonable. A few sites are extremely popular, but most receive only a small number of visits. Gene Stanley of Boston University, and editor of *Physica A*, the world's leading statistical physics journal, examined with his colleague Luis Amaral the pattern of sexual contacts. They found that this, too, had scale-free properties. A relatively small number of people had a high number of contacts, and most people had a small number.

This might be considered as either amusing or esoteric (or both). But there are highly practical policy implications. We discussed above networks in which people are more or less equally likely to meet any other individual. These, too, seem to exist in social and economic life. Remember that in such networks there is a critical point relating to the percentage of the population that becomes infected. Below this level, a virus will die off of its own accord. Above this level, it will spread rapidly through the population. Scale-free networks have a critical point of zero! In other words, in such networks *any* virus, no matter how few it has infected, might disseminate across the population. It is important to note that this does not mean that it necessarily will. But in principle it can.

These differences imply markedly different policies for successful inoculation. In the first kind, inoculating a particular percentage of the population purely at random has a high probability of success. The task of identifying this critical percentage might be difficult in practice, but theoretically it is straightforward to show that it exists. A current practical illustration in the UK is the heated debate over the triple MMR vaccine. Rightly or wrongly, many parents are becoming convinced that the vaccine in this form may trigger autism in children. The British government insists that this is not the case and refuses to give the inoculations in three single jabs. Given the nature of the diseases being combated in this way, such as measles, it is not unreasonable to think of them as being spread by random social contact, like the common cold. So there is a serious worry that the percentage of inoculated children might drop below the critical threshold.

In contrast, in a scale-free network random inoculation, even of a high percentage of the relevant population, has only a low probability of success. The major disseminators, the very small number of highly connected individuals, may easily slip through such a net. To be effective, policies of containment need to target these select few and neutralise their influence.

How many crimes do individuals commit?

Criminologists have made some progress in identifying individuals who are more likely to become criminals (at some point in their lives) than others. Being born into a family where most members are criminals increases this probability substantially. And it is now clear that boys raised by single-parent, never-married mothers also exhibit a higher probability of being involved in crime than others with different family backgrounds.

But it is neither practical nor appropriate to imprison boys from criminal families as soon as they reach puberty, still less to incarcerate every boy from a poor, single-parent family. Could we not instead attempt to identify the much smaller number of those who are likely to commit large numbers of crimes and devote resources to try to switch their behaviour away from such a path before it is too late? From our understanding of scale-free networks, this policy might be effective.

If we could do so, there would be a double impact on crime. First, a reduction in the crimes committed by these individuals and, second, a weakening of the influence of criminality as a social norm among their peers. Individuals undoubtedly attract attention and gain influence in such social circles if they are known to have committed large numbers of crimes.

Surprisingly, there is relatively little systematic work on the number of crimes committed by individuals. But there are two databases that record criminality by particular individuals over time. The first, the Cambridge Study in Delinquent Development, is a prospective longitudinal survey of 411 males in a working-class area of North London. Data collection began in 1961/62. The second, the Pittsburgh Youth Study, began in 1986 with a random sample of boys in the first, fourth and seventh grades of the Pittsburgh, Pennsylvania, public school system. The sample contains approximately 500 boys at each grade level, for a total of 1,517 boys. Most crime is committed by young men, and both the Cambridge and the Pittsburgh studies monitor behaviour over time in groups of youths.

The Cambridge data relates to the number of convictions for each boy over a period spanning the mid-1960s and 1970s. The Pittsburgh data describes self-reported acts of delinquency over short time intervals beginning in the late 1980s. In other words, the studies differ both in their time coverage and in the fact that the Cambridge study describes convictions for offences and the Pittsburgh one describes self-reported acts of delinquency.

Despite the fact that the two databases examine different aspects of criminal activity – convictions and self-reported acts of delinquency – over different timescales, there is a remarkable similarity between the two in the statistical distribution of the number of crimes associated with individuals. The 'statistical distribution' in this context describes how many individuals in each database commit (or record) zero crime, how many commit just one, how many commit two, and so on.

The actual analysis relies on a number of mathematical concepts that would take considerable time to describe in plain English. For those interested in the details, I have published the analysis in a paper (Ormerod et al., 2004).[1]

There are two striking features of the results. First, a much better description of the number of crimes committed by individuals is given if we segment the number into two separate groups than if we analyse them together. Specifically, the groups are 'the numbers who commit zero crimes' and 'the numbers who commit any crime'. In other words, the description of the data when the numbers of boys committing or reporting zero crimes are excluded is different from that when they are included.

---

1   It may be thought unusual that a statistical physics journal would be interested in this analysis, but the statistical distribution identified is one of general interest to this particular research community.

Second, once this distinction is made there is no 'typical' number of crimes that an individual commits. Once a boy has moved from committing no crime to committing just one crime, the total number of criminal acts he might commit can take place on all scales. Moreover, the number of crimes that any individual does in fact commit can be thought of as the outcome of a purely random process.

These are abstract concepts but they have an important practical implication – namely, the fact that the number of crimes committed by an individual is compatible with the outcome of a purely random process means that it is not possible to identify in advance, once a crime has been committed, how many crimes that individual will go on to commit. So we cannot hope to target *in advance* those boys who will have a highly prolific career in crime, and who may therefore exercise a strong influence over the behaviour of their peers. We may, as discussed above, be able to go some way in identifying those who are more likely to make the first crucial step from zero to one crime, but we cannot then go on to identify who will commit many more crimes and those whose criminal career will involve only a small number.

This evidence fits very neatly with the properties of the model of how crime evolves described by Figure 4. An important property of such models is that the single most effective place to intervene in terms of reducing the number of individuals in the hard-core *C* category is in fact the flow, not directly in and out of *C* itself, but from the *N* to the *S* category – in other words, from those not interested in crime to those who commit the occasional crime and now have the potential to graduate into hardened criminals. Analysis of the Cambridge and Pittsburgh databases shows that the distinction between those who commit no crime and those who commit one is also crucial. Once an individual has committed one crime, he may go on to commit any number of crimes.

6 WHAT CAN WE CONCLUDE?

All this may seem complex and hard to understand. This statement is true in several ways. We are dealing with developments that are at the frontiers of science in terms of the application of the insights of graph theory to practical social and economic situations. And earlier in this essay, we noted the remarks of economics Nobel laureate Daniel Kahneman to the effect that incorporating non-traditional but more realistic modes of behaviour into economic theory presents difficult challenges.

The existing literature on crime offers some understanding of the process by which it is generated and by which it spreads. But our level of comprehension, offered by traditional approaches, is very limited. Economics has made an important contribution in emphasising the impact of incentives, both positive and negative, on behaviour. There is, however, strong evidence that criminals, and those likely to indulge in criminal behaviour, do not behave as completely rationally as economic theory postulates they should.

Further, crime does not arise from the behaviour of Robinson Crusoes, of individuals operating in isolation and calculating their optimal self-interested course of action. People live in society, and the actions of other individuals may serve as role models and alter their behaviour, for good or for ill. We are beginning to discover how the kind of social network in which individuals are connected – and this will differ in different contexts – can be of crucial importance in designing effective strategies of containment.

A key reason for writing this monograph is that many existing models, particularly econometric ones, will produce perfectly refined quantitative predictions that are qualitatively wrong! In contrast, models of the kind discussed above are often more successful in terms of their qualitative predictions, even though it is very difficult to attach a magnitude to them. But, as Hayek noted many years ago, it is far better to have the correct conclusions but be unsure of the magnitudes than to appear to quantify something precisely which is at best spurious and at worst misleading.

Tentative as the conclusion must be, a policy implication that is hard to avoid is the need to restore non-criminal behaviour as the social norm among relatively deprived young men. Currently, around 20 per cent of this social group during any given year either commit burglary or are in prison for it. And to this number must be added those whose penchant is merely for crimes of theft or violence. Patterns of social restraint have clearly broken down. Rather like Humpty Dumpty, putting them back together again is by no means an easy task. Indeed, the analysis shows that strategies to reduce crime are by no means as straightforward as many practitioners imagine, and strategies of detailed intervention and planning have only low probabilities of success. Further, the influence of government may be rather complex. Nevertheless, some important conclusions do seem clear from the theory and evidence.

There seems little point in giving short prison sentences to repeat offenders, particularly to those whose deeds give them prestige in their communities. Much longer sentences for prominent individuals could exercise a deterrent effect, not necessarily mainly among the already criminal, but among those who are not committing crime themselves.

Preventing an individual from taking the first critical step of committing a single crime is crucial in containing the overall crime rate. Deterrence can only be part of the policy, though it is hard to rationalise either the sharp falls in crime in America over the past ten years or so or the large increases that have taken place in the UK over the past half-century without concluding that this must have played a role.

Policies of rehabilitating hard-core criminals have had little success, even though a wide variety has been tried, and in any event are of very much second order of importance compared with the need to deter individuals from committing their very first crime.

The group of those boys from poor backgrounds who have so far committed no crime is the group that it is particularly important to influence. In addition to deterrence, we must attempt to restore social norms so that it ceases to be acceptable to drift into a life of crime.

Any list of possible positive influences on social norms is open to scepticism or derision, depending upon the political perspective of the critic. But the development of role models and the influence of voluntary organisations both seem important. Legislation that encourages the never-married single-mother family is not very sensible. This judgement is not made on moral grounds, but because it increases very substantially the probability of the boys being in the category 'low skilled and poor', which group in turn supplies the bulk of criminals. But it is only after the event that this has become clear – again illustrating the difficulties of predicting strategies to reduce crime in advance.

This complexity, inherent in the factors that we have modelled and in their interactions, together with the difficulty of selecting effective strategies in advance, means that competition among and imitation of effective policies are important. In other words, we need to filter effective policies through a process of discovery and experimentation. More local government autonomy from central government, for example, in the area of crime and policing, would be helpful because this could lead to a wider variety of policies being tried.

Less welcome to free-market economists is the conclusion that, as an economic influence, the minimum wage appears to have restrained crime. Substantial increases in its rate raise wider economic issues which need careful balancing, but the potential savings to society through reduced levels of crime are large as long as the minimum wage does not substantially increase unemployment among the potential criminal group.

Overall, a combination of 21st-century economic theory and 21st-century social network analysis offers the potential for a much better understanding of crime. I do not even pretend to claim that I have accomplished the task in this essay. But I hope to have illustrated how we can build on the value of conventional economics, extending it both with more realistic models of behaviour and by placing individuals in a social context. By combining in analytical models the insights of both economic theory and sociology, we will be able to devise much more successful practical strategies for the containment of crime.

REFERENCES

Allan, E. and D. Steffensmeier (1989), 'Youth, underemployment, and property crime: effects of the quantity and the quality of job opportunities on juvenile and young adult arrest rates', *American Sociological Review*, 54: 107–23

Cook, W. and P. Ormerod (2003), 'Non-linearity and local interaction in area crime rates in the United States', prepared for the Institute for Complex Additive Systems Analysis of the New Mexico Institute of Mining and Technology

Currie, E. (1996), *Is America Really Winning the War on Crime and Should Britain Follow Its Example?*, London: NACRO

Ehrlich, I. (1996), 'Crime, punishment and the market for offences', *Journal of Economic Perspectives*, 10, 1: 43–67

Glaeser, E. L., B. Sacerdote and J. A. Scheinkman (1996), 'Crime and social interactions', *Quarterly Journal of Economics*, CXI(2): 507–48

Gould, E., B. Weinberg and D. Mustard (2002), 'Crime rates and local labour market opportunities in the United States: 1979–1995', *Review of Economics and Statistics*, 84: 45–61

Hansen, K. and S. Machin (2003), 'Modelling crime at police force area level', Home Office Occasional Paper no. 80, section E, London: Home Office

Kahneman, D. (2003), 'Maps of bounded rationality: psychology for behavioral economics', *American Economic Review*, 93: 1449–75

Levitt, S. and L. Lochner (2001), 'The determinants of juvenile crime', in J. Gruber (ed.), *Risky Behavior among Youths: An Economic Analysis*, Chicago: University of Chicago Press

Marris, R. L. (2003), *Survey of the Research Literature on the Economic and Criminological Factors Influencing Crime Trends*, London: Home Office

Murray, J. D. (1990), *Mathematical Biology*, Springer Verlag

Ormerod, P., W. Cook and E. Cooper (2004), 'Scaling behaviour in the number of criminal acts committed by individuals', *Journal of Statistical Mechanics: Theory and Experiment*, July

Ormerod, P., L. Smith and C. Mounfield (2003), 'Nonlinear modelling of burglary and violent crime in the UK', Home Office Occasional Paper no. 80, section B, London: Home Office

Raphael, S. and R. Winter-Ebmer (2001), 'Identifying the effect of male unemployment on crime', *Journal of Law and Economics*, 44: 259–84

ABOUT THE IEA

The Institute is a research and educational charity (No. CC 235 351), limited by guarantee. Its mission is to improve understanding of the fundamental institutions of a free society with particular reference to the role of markets in solving economic and social problems.

The IEA achieves its mission by:

- a high-quality publishing programme
- conferences, seminars, lectures and other events
- outreach to school and college students
- brokering media introductions and appearances

The IEA, which was established in 1955 by the late Sir Antony Fisher, is an educational charity, not a political organisation. It is independent of any political party or group and does not carry on activities intended to affect support for any political party or candidate in any election or referendum, or at any other time. It is financed by sales of publications, conference fees and voluntary donations.

In addition to its main series of publications the IEA also publishes a quarterly journal, *Economic Affairs*, and has two specialist programmes – Environment and Technology, and Education.

The IEA is aided in its work by a distinguished international Academic Advisory Council and an eminent panel of Honorary Fellows. Together with other academics, they review prospective IEA publications, their comments being passed on anonymously to authors. All IEA papers are therefore subject to the same rigorous independent refereeing process as used by leading academic journals.

IEA publications enjoy widespread classroom use and course adoptions in schools and universities. They are also sold throughout the world and often translated/reprinted.

Since 1974 the IEA has helped to create a world-wide network of 100 similar institutions in over 70 countries. They are all independent but share the IEA's mission.

Views expressed in the IEA's publications are those of the authors, not those of the Institute (which has no corporate view), its Managing Trustees, Academic Advisory Council members or senior staff.

Members of the Institute's Academic Advisory Council, Honorary Fellows, Trustees and Staff are listed on the following page.

The Institute gratefully acknowledges financial support for its publications programme and other work from a generous benefaction by the late Alec and Beryl Warren.

93

Other papers recently published by the IEA include:

WHO, What and Why?

Transnational Government, Legitimacy and the World Health Organization
Roger Scruton
Occasional Paper 113; ISBN 0 255 36487 3
£8.00

The World Turned Rightside Up

A New Trading Agenda for the Age of Globalisation
John C. Hulsman
Occasional Paper 114; ISBN 0 255 36495 4
£8.00

The Representation of Business in English Literature

Introduced and edited by Arthur Pollard
Readings 53; ISBN 0 255 36491 1
£12.00

Anti-Liberalism 2000

The Rise of New Millennium Collectivism
David Henderson
Occasional Paper 115; ISBN 0 255 36497 0
£7.50

Capitalism, Morality and Markets

Brian Griffiths, Robert A. Sirico, Norman Barry & Frank Field
Readings 54; ISBN 0 255 36496 2
£7.50

A Conversation with Harris and Seldon

Ralph Harris & Arthur Seldon
Occasional Paper 116; ISBN 0 255 36498 9
£7.50

Malaria and the DDT Story

Richard Tren & Roger Bate
Occasional Paper 117; ISBN 0 255 36499 7
£10.00

A Plea to Economists Who Favour Liberty: Assist the Everyman

Daniel B. Klein
Occasional Paper 118; ISBN 0 255 36501 2
£10.00

The Changing Fortunes of Economic Liberalism

Yesterday, Today and Tomorrow
David Henderson
Occasional Paper 105 (new edition); ISBN 0 255 36520 9
£12.50

The Global Education Industry

Lessons from Private Education in Developing Countries
James Tooley
Hobart Paper 141 (new edition); ISBN 0 255 36503 9
£12.50

Saving Our Streams

*The Role of the Anglers' Conservation Association in
Protecting English and Welsh Rivers*
Roger Bate
Research Monograph 53; ISBN 0 255 36494 6
£10.00

Better Off Out?

The Benefits or Costs of EU Membership
Brian Hindley & Martin Howe
Occasional Paper 99 (new edition); ISBN 0 255 36502 0
£10.00

Buckingham at 25

Freeing the Universities from State Control
Edited by James Tooley
Readings 55; ISBN 0 255 36512 8
£15.00

Lectures on Regulatory and Competition Policy

Irwin M. Stelzer

Occasional Paper 120; ISBN 0 255 36511 X

£12.50

Misguided Virtue

False Notions of Corporate Social Responsibility

David Henderson

Hobart Paper 142; ISBN 0 255 36510 1

£12.50

HIV and Aids in Schools

The Political Economy of Pressure Groups and Miseducation

Barrie Craven, Pauline Dixon, Gordon Stewart & James Tooley

Occasional Paper 121; ISBN 0 255 36522 5

£10.00

The Road to Serfdom

The Reader's Digest *condensed version*

Friedrich A. Hayek

Occasional Paper 122; ISBN 0 255 36530 6

£7.50

Bastiat's *The Law*

Introduction by Norman Barry

Occasional Paper 123; ISBN 0 255 36509 8

£7.50

A Globalist Manifesto for Public Policy

Charles Calomiris

Occasional Paper 124; ISBN 0 255 36525 X

£7.50

Euthanasia for Death Duties

Putting Inheritance Tax Out of Its Misery

Barry Bracewell-Milnes

Research Monograph 54; ISBN 0 255 36513 6

£10.00

Liberating the Land

The Case for Private Land-use Planning

Mark Pennington

Hobart Paper 143; ISBN 0 255 36508 X

£10.00

IEA Yearbook of Government Performance 2002/2003
Edited by Peter Warburton
Yearbook 1; ISBN 0 255 36532 2
£15.00

Britain's Relative Economic Performance, 1870–1999
Nicholas Crafts
Research Monograph 55; ISBN 0 255 36524 1
£10.00

Should We Have Faith in Central Banks?
Otmar Issing
Occasional Paper 125; ISBN 0 255 36528 4
£7.50

The Dilemma of Democracy
Arthur Seldon
Hobart Paper 136 (reissue); ISBN 0 255 36536 5
£10.00

Capital Controls: a 'Cure' Worse Than the Problem?
Forrest Capie
Research Monograph 56; ISBN 0 255 36506 3
£10.00

The Poverty of 'Development Economics'

Deepak Lal

Hobart Paper 144 (reissue); ISBN 0 255 36519 5

£15.00

Should Britain Join the Euro?

The Chancellor's Five Tests Examined

Patrick Minford

Occasional Paper 126; ISBN 0 255 36527 6

£7.50

Post-Communist Transition: Some Lessons

Leszek Balcerowicz

Occasional Paper 127; ISBN 0 255 36533 0

£7.50

A Tribute to Peter Bauer

John Blundell et al.

Occasional Paper 128; ISBN 0 255 36531 4

£10.00

Employment Tribunals

Their Growth and the Case for Radical Reform

J. R. Shackleton

Hobart Paper 145; ISBN 0 255 36515 2

£10.00

Fifty Economic Fallacies Exposed

Geoffrey E. Wood
Occasional Paper 129; ISBN 0 255 36518 7
£12.50

A Market in Airport Slots

Keith Boyfield (editor), David Starkie, Tom Bass & Barry Humphreys
Readings 56; ISBN 0 255 36505 5
£10.00

Money, Inflation and the Constitutional Position of the Central Bank

Milton Friedman & Charles A. E. Goodhart
Readings 57; ISBN 0 255 36538 1
£10.00

railway.com

Parallels between the Early British Railways and the ICT Revolution
Robert C. B. Miller
Research Monograph 57; ISBN 0 255 36534 9
£12.50

The Regulation of Financial Markets

Edited by Philip Booth & David Currie
Readings 58; ISBN 0 255 36551 9
£12.50

Climate Alarmism Reconsidered

Robert L. Bradley Jr

Hobart Paper 146; ISBN 0 255 36541 1

£12.50

Government Failure: E. G. West on Education

Edited by James Tooley & James Stanfield

Occasional Paper 130; ISBN 0 255 36552 7

£12.50

Waging the War of Ideas

John Blundell

Second edition

Occasional Paper 131; ISBN 0 255 36547 0

£12.50

Corporate Governance: Accountability in the Marketplace

Elaine Sternberg

Second edition

Hobart Paper 147; ISBN 0 255 36542 X

£12.50

The Land Use Planning System
Evaluating Options for Reform
John Corkindale
Hobart Paper 148; ISBN 0 255 36550 0
£10.00

Economy and Virtue
Essays on the Theme of Markets and Morality
Edited by Dennis O'Keeffe
Readings 59; ISBN 0 255 36504 7
£12.50

Free Markets Under Siege
Cartels, Politics and Social Welfare
Richard A. Epstein
Occasional Paper 132; ISBN 0 255 36553 5
£10.00

Unshackling Accountants
D. R. Myddelton
Hobart Paper 149; ISBN 0 255 36559 4
£12.50

The Euro as Politics
Pedro Schwartz
Research Monograph 58; ISBN 0 255 36535 7
£12.50

Pricing Our Roads

Vision and Reality
Stephen Glaister & Daniel J. Graham
Research Monograph 59; ISBN 0 255 36562 4
£10.00

The Role of Business in the Modern World

Progress, Pressures, and Prospects for the Market Economy
David Henderson
Hobart Paper 150; ISBN 0 255 36548 9
£12.50

Public Service Broadcasting Without the BBC?

Alan Peacock
Occasional Paper 133; ISBN 0 255 36565 9
£10.00

The ECB and the Euro: the First Five Years

Otmar Issing
Occasional Paper 134; ISBN 0 255 36555 1
£10.00

Towards a Liberal Utopia?

Edited by Philip Booth
Hobart Paperback 32; ISBN 0 255 36563 2
£15.00

The Way Out of the Pensions Quagmire

Philip Booth & Deborah Cooper

Research Monograph 60; ISBN 0 255 36517 9

£12.50

Black Wednesday

A Re-examination of Britain's Experience in the Exchange Rate Mechanism

Alan Budd

Occasional Paper 135; ISBN 0 255 36566 7

£7.50

To order copies of currently available IEA papers, or to enquire about availability, please contact:

Lavis Marketing
IEA orders
FREEPOST LON21280
Oxford OX3 7BR

Tel: 01865 767575
Fax: 01865 750079
Email: orders@lavismarketing.co.uk

The IEA also offers a subscription service to its publications. For a single annual payment, currently £40.00 in the UK, you will receive every title the IEA publishes during the course of a year, invitations to events, and discounts on our extensive back catalogue. For more information, please contact:

Adam Myers
Subscriptions
The Institute of Economic Affairs
2 Lord North Street
London SW1P 3LB

Tel: 020 7799 8920
Fax: 020 7799 2137
Website: www.iea.org.uk